DATE DUE

Women's Rights in Old Testament Times

JAMES R. BAKER

Signature Books
Salt Lake City
1992

cover design: Julie Easton

Composed and printed in the United States of America.
96   95   94   93   92   6   5   4   3   2   1

LIBRARY OF CONGRESS CATALOGING-IN-PUBLICATION DATA
Baker, James R.
    Women's rights in Old Testament Times / James R. Baker.
        p.   cm.
    Includes bibliographical references and index.
    ISBN 1-56085-029-9
    1. Women in the Bible. 2. Bible. O.T.—Criticism,
interpretation, etc. 3. Jewish law—Sources. 4. Women—Legal
status, laws, etc. (Jewish law) I. Title.
BS575.B28   1992
221.9'5'082—dc   92-4953
                                                            CIP

To my father, Al Baker,
who, apart from my wife,
is my best friend
and has been an inspiration to me
all my life.

CONTENTS

CONTENTS

PREFACE

People's lives generally reflect the social norms of their times, some of which find expression in codified law. Deciphering stories of ancient Hebrew women requires cultural sophistica-tion, especially an understanding of their usually murky back-drop. Although women are partly concealed by the patriarchal emphasis of the Bible, they exerted considerable influence in their communities and were often adept at working the law to their advantage.

The study of ancient Israel has long been the province of religious scholars, one of whom observed, "Biblical Law is too important to be left to lawyers."[1] But after looking to the puzzling social and historical context of Hebrew women, I discovered a void and have decided to take on the task myself.

One incidental point of interest to me as a lawyer is the consistency between the Bible and what I can discover of contemporaneous, external legal codes. This affirms for me that the Hebrew Bible was written by scribes who lived at or near the times they were describing, whatever the historicity of any particular story. Historians and theologians continue this debate.

There are several limitations to understanding ancient law,

not the least of which is linguistic. No one has spoken Akkadian or Sumerian or written in cuneiform or hieroglyphics for centuries. Scholarly debate continues over the accuracy of various translations. For example, who is a *muskenum* versus an *awelum* in the Code of Hammurabi? The context makes it clear that these are class distinctions, but their comparative status cannot be determined. Laws and punishments were administered differently for a nobleman than for a commoner, for a temple priestess than for a matron.

I rely heavily on the opinions of Middle Eastern scholars who have made the study of ancient legal texts their lifelong vocation. Not surprisingly, there are significant debates over most major legal theories and principles. What exactly was a concubine? How was the first born chosen? My guiding principle has been to prefer conclusions which most reasonably explain the narratives without textual manipulation.

There are other interpretive difficulties, including chronological contradictions, little surviving information about legal customs in some countries, the borrowing of legal theory from one country by another and from one century to the next,[2] the rendering of judgment in the absence of law or in spite of the law due to political realities,[3] and the scarcity of nomadic as opposed to urban law. In addition, so little is recorded about some women that next to nothing can be deduced at all. I also omit consideration of Deborah, Esther, and others because their stories do not involve legal issues.

Unless otherwise noted, all scriptural quotations are from the King James Version of the Bible. I have elected to use this translation due to its popularity rather than its interpretive superiority. In quoting translations of legal documents, I used French brackets to add material, allowing translators and editors their standard brackets and parentheses for lacunae and clarifications. Outside of quotations from other authors' commentaries, I use parentheses.

I should also add that I am not a student of feminist theory, although the potential significance of my work to women's studies is hopefully apparent. Finally, readers should note what I see as one overall theme of the Bible: the inevitable downfall of the arrogant by those less privileged and more deserving. Implicit here is an acknowledgment that all was not rosy for women of ancient times. But they were protected in some rights and asserted themselves in other areas, sometimes heroically.

Publication of this book is the culmination of a fifteen-year dream. During that time many people assisted me. In particular, I appreciate Doug Parker, my mentor in law school, who aided me in other classes when I persisted in writing papers on ancient legal principles instead of current issues. I am grateful to David Thomas and the library staff of the J. Reuben Clark Law School, as well as to Doug Gould and the staff of the Harold B. Lee library, for research privileges granted me. Assistance provided by Anna and Dick Jacobsen, Joy Rigby, and Margaret Sanders is also appreciated. Lavina Fielding Anderson was very helpful in reviewing, critiquing, and editing the text; and I owe a debt of gratitude to her. Most of all, I cannot begin to express my gratitude for my wife who sacrificed financially and remained cheerful through some very trying times. Lastly, I would like to express appreciation for a Supreme Creator, in whom I have a firm conviction and without whose support I would not have attempted such an undertaking.

The above notwithstanding, I alone am responsible for any errors in this work.

Notes

1. Bernard S. Jackson, "The Ceremonial and Judicial: Biblical Law as Sign and Symbol," *Journal of Studies in the Old Testament* 30 (1984): 25.

2. G. R. Driver and J. C. Miles claim: "When, then, the

Old-Accadian Laws are compared on the one hand with the Laws of Hammurabi and on the other hand with the Sumerian and Middle-Assyrian Laws and perhaps also with those of the Hebrews, the conclusion that there was a common customary law throughout the Fertile Crescent seems irresistible; and this common law was to a considerable extent written law" (*The Babylonian Laws*, 2 vols. [1952; reprt. Oxford: Oxford University Press, 1968], 1:9). E. Neufeld, an expert on ancient Hittite law, states, "With regard to the type of their substance, structure, legal scope, technical presentation and arrangement of subject matter, the collection of Hittite laws shows, on the surface, a remarkable degree of uniformity with the LE [laws of Eshnunna], LH [laws of Hammurabi], the Assyrian law tablets and the legal documents contained in the Old Testament" (*The Hittite Laws* [London: Luzac & Co., 1951], 101). Of course, even where there are such stark similarities, the contrast with modern Western legal traditions is enormous.

3. Maimonides recorded an irrigation law that recognized the priority of water rights for landowners who were physically stronger. Isaac Klein, trans., *The Book of Acquisitions*, Book 12 of *The Code of Maimonides* (New Haven, CT: Yale University Press, 1951), 170.

I.

Twelve Ancient Legal Documents

What are the known ancient laws that dominated the Old Testament world? Here follows a brief discussion of twelve of the most important:

Code of Ur-Nammu	ca. 2200 B.C.
Sumerian Laws	ca. 2200-1800 B.C.
Laws of Eshnunna	ca. 1900 B.C.
Code of Lipit-Ishtar	ca. 1800 B.C.
Code of Hammurabi (Old Babylonian)	ca. 1700 B.C.
The Edict of Ammisaduqa	ca. 1600 B.C.
Middle Assyrian Laws	ca. 1400 B.C.
Hittite Laws	ca. 1300 B.C.
Nuzi Law	ca. 1300 B.C.
Mosaic Law	ca. 1200 B.C.
Neo-Babylonian Laws	ca. 600 B.C.
Jewish Law	ca. A.D. 200-600

Ancient legal texts, called "codes" or "codices," are not to be confused with the sophisticated legal codes of modern Europe or even classical Rome, for their purposes were different. Ancient legal codes are rough compilations of legal ab-

1

stracts of the king's rulings or those of his courts recorded to
show posterity that the king had fulfilled his mandate to bestow
justice and equity upon the poor, the widowed, the orphaned,
and the enslaved.[1] These laws were apparently not as binding
as they were instructive of what one could reasonably expect.[2]

They also served as exercises in scribal schools, exercises
which helped preserve much of the cultural and literary inheritance of the ancient Near East.[3] Perhaps most important for
our purposes, the law throughout the Fertile Crescent was for
most practical purposes universal, and the legal principles
underlying the various codes were basically the same.[4]

The Code Of Ur-nammu

Ur-Nammu was the king and founding ruler of the third
dynasty of Ur, comprising the city and region of Sumeria, the
southern portion of Mesopotamia. He also built the best
preserved ziggurat in Mesopotamia.[5] The Ur-Nammu Codex
is the oldest known legal code, dated variously from the middle
to the end of the third millennium B.C.[6]

The code was found in two sources, both damaged and
incomplete. The first was a poorly preserved tablet discovered
at Nippur and translated from Sumerian by Samuel N. Kramer in 1954.[7] The second source was two pieces of a tablet
that seems to have been the work of a student scribe and was
left unfinished. This text was found in Ur and translated by
O. R. Gurney and Samuel Kramer in 1965.[8] Due to their
poor condition, the tablets spent fifty years in a warehouse
before they were deciphered and their importance realized. I
use the translation of J. J. Finkelstein, who revised and
continued Kramer's translations.[9]

Most of the prologue to the codex has been lost, but the
surviving fragments report that Ur-Nammu was the "son born
of {the goddess} Ninsun," that he was a pious supporter of

the temple, that he had freed up trade by establishing equity in the land, and that he protected the widowed, the orphaned, and the "man of one shekel."[10]

Much of the section on laws has been lost or badly damaged, but what remains deals among other things with adultery of a married woman, the defloration of someone else's female slave, divorce and alimony, false accusation, the escape of slaves, the status of slaves, bodily injury, the granting of security, and legal cases arising from agriculture and irrigation.

Section eleven—the most bizarre and the harshest for women—requires a wife accused by a man other than her husband of adultery to prove her innocence by ordeal—leaping into the river (presumably the Euphrates). If she is guilty she drowns. If she survives her accuser pays her husband twenty shekels of silver. The code provides some protection for wives. A divorcing husband had to pay his wife one mina (sixty shekels) of silver, which was sufficient to purchase at least three slaves (sec. 6).

This early code used conditional phrasing ("if a man" or "suppose that a man"), a legal convention that became the norm for all ancient Near Eastern precedent law.[11] The same phrasing appears in the Code of Lipit-Ishtar and the Code of Hammurabi, suggesting that the Code of Ur-Nammu was their forerunner.

The Sumerian Laws

The background of the Sumerian laws is the least clear of any I deal with. In 1915 A. T. Clay published nine laws found on a large tablet at Erech (Uruk), northwest of Ur in southern Mesopotamia.[12] Clay tentatively dated it to 2200-1800 B.C. Clay believed that the laws were those of a pre-Hammurabic ruler from the Lagash-Nippur area. However, current opinion,

3

held by Finkelstein and others, is that a student in a scribal school of southern Mesopotamia made the compilation from an unknown source.[13] It predates Hammurabi, which borrows some of its linguistic formulae.[14]

The nine laws cover such issues as the abuse of pregnant women, negligent loss of a boat, disinheritance, and the rape of a freeman's daughter.

The sections dealing with abuse of pregnant women focus on intent. If a woman miscarried because a man "jostled" her but did not mean harm, he was fined ten shekels. But if he "smote" her, intending to cause harm, the fine was twenty shekels (secs. 1, 2).

Sections 7 and 8 deal with the rape of a virgin. If the rapist knew that his victim was a freeman's daughter, the father could force him to marry her. If the rapist swore that he did not know her status, he did not have to marry her or pay a fine. Later codes such as the Middle Assyrian Laws (sec. A 55) removed this unfortunate loophole.

The Laws of Eshnunna

Eshnunna was north of Ur on the Tigris River and became politically important after the fall of the third dynasty of Ur, founded by Ur-Nammu. The Iraq Directorate of Antiquities found two parallel sets of tablets in 1945 and 1947 at Tell Abu Harmal near Baghdad. Albrecht Goetze of Yale University first translated them from Akkadian and published them in 1948.[15]

The laws concern marriage, matrimonial offenses, divorce, slaves and slave children, contracts, property, and various wrongs or injuries—all without much systematization, order, or structure.[16] Sometimes a statute is most troublesome because of its omissions. For example, section 24 concerns the detainment and injury of the wife or child of a freeman against whom the perpetrator has no claim even though he may believe he has. If the wife or child dies from abuse, the perpetrator is executed. This leaves open the question of whether a creditor could legally seize and torture the family of a debtor.

Another interesting provision of this code is section 59, which discourages men from abandoning their wives, after they had borne children. In such cases, the woman receives all of her husband's property.

The more structured and carefully compiled Code of Hammurabi contains a high proportion of technical and semi-technical terms that are similar to the Laws of Eshnunna— for example, those depicting concepts of negligence or the methodology of stating claims. About 75 percent of the Laws of Eshnunna reappear without much change in the Code of Hammurabi—evidence that the later compiler knew the earlier code.[17]

The Lipit-Ishtar Code

King Lipit-Ishtar reigned eleven years as the fifth ruler of the dynasty of Isin, a Babylonian city-state south of Babylon, before the unification under Hammurabi in the eighteenth century B.C.[18] Lipit-Ishtar predated Hammurabi. Although his dates are disputed, he probably ruled sometime between 1900 and 1800 B.C.[19]

An expedition from the University of Pennsylvania uncovered four tablet fragments in Nippur during 1889-1900. These fragments were stored with about 3,000 other tablets until about 1939 when Samuel Kramer and Francis Steele of the University Museum at the University of Pennsylvania took note of them, matching them with a brief collection of seventeen laws from three Nippur fragments that F. Lutz of the University Museum had published in 1919.

A fourth piece, making eight in all, had been published in 1929 by H. de Genouillac, who had found it in the Louvre.

Steele put the puzzle together and published the Code of Lipit-Ishtar in 1948.[20] The fragments reveal about four hundred lines of an original tablet that contained an estimated twelve hundred lines[21]

In the remnant of the prologue, Lipit-Ishtar claims to have brought well-being and justice to Sumer and Akkad (later Babylonia), a claim similar to that made by Hammurabi. He also claims to have freed his people from slavery and reestablished such equitable family practices as requiring fathers to support young children and the children to support aging fathers.[22]

The laws include thirty-eight sections from the second half of the code dealing with real estate, servitude, interest rates (ranging from 20 percent to 33.3 percent), inheritance, marriage, and penalties for damages to or caused by rented oxen.

It has several innovative provisions. For example, it is the first legal code to deal substantively with the inheritances of children of plural wives, including slave wives and prostitutes. It is also the first to allow daughters to inherit from fathers, but the examples seem limited to daughters dedicated to a temple (sec. 22). Since this is the only code without a specific clause on divorce, it may be assumed that it is among the eight hundred lost lines.

The code ends with a long epilogue, which reads in part: "I, Lipit-Ishtar, the son of Enlil, {the storm god} abolished enmity and rebellion; made weeping, lamentations, outcries . . . taboo; caused righteousness and truth to exist; brought well-being to the Sumerians and the Akkadians."[23] He concludes by blessing those who do not damage his stela and cursing those who do, a pattern followed by Hammurabi.[24]

The Code of Hammurabi

The most famous, complete, and best preserved ancient legal text is that of Hammurabi, the sixth of eleven kings of the

Old Babylonian dynasty,[25] dating from approximately 1850 to 1550 B.C. His was a reign graced by academic achievement evidenced by grammatical texts, dictionaries, mathematical treatises more sophisticated than any by the Greeks, astronomical understanding, and more.[26] During his forty-three-year reign, he consolidated the Babylonian empire and had a cylindrical diorite monument inscribed with a frieze depicting himself paying homage to Shamash, the sun-god who was also the god of justice. Engraved around the cylindrical monument was a prologue, a code of laws, and an epilogue.

V. Scheil discovered this monument during the winter of 1901-1902 while he was excavating the ancient site of Susa (the biblical city of Esther and Daniel) located east of Babylon across the Tigris River in modern Iran. It had probably been carried there by a ruler who had successfully sacked Babylon.[27]

The prologue reads:

> At that time Anum {sky-god and leader of the pan-
> theon} and Enlil named me
> to promote the welfare of the people,
> me, Hammurabi, the devout, god-fearing prince,
> to cause justice to prevail in the land,
> to destroy the wicked and the evil,
> that the strong might not oppress the weak,
> to rise like the sun over the black-headed (people),
> and light up the land.
> Hammurabi, the shepherd, called by Enlil am I.[28]

In general the 282-section code deals with crimes, real property, commerce, marriage, inheritance, priestesses, adoption, assault, agriculture, wages, slaves, and courts. The code specifies a three-year time limit on slavery for debt, which provides an interesting comparison to the Mosaic law's six-year limit on slavery for debt. Of particular interest are laws protecting gifts of real property to wife and daughter, requirements that marriage contracts be written, and automatic freedom at a master's death for a slave who has given birth to his children.

The code, while showing signs of enlightenment, is not without some barbarism. If a woman goes into business, neglects her household, and humiliates her husband, the husband may either divorce her without compensation or marry another wife and make the first a slave.[29]

This code is the first to suggest that a woman has a right to divorce, but she must prove that her husband is unworthy. If she is found at fault instead, she is executed.[30]

This code is the most complete of the ancient world, but it was apparently not intended to be all-inclusive nor binding in the sense of modern codes but rather to give direction and representative verdicts of justice. According to its epilogue, its purpose is "to make justice to appear in the land, to destroy the evil and the wicked, [in order] that the strong might not oppress the weak."[31] Some of the code was erased, presumably by a subsequent ruler in Susa who perhaps intended to add his own achievements.[32] The erasures include sections 66-99, some of which have been found in other poorly preserved sources.[33]

In the epilogue Hammurabi calls himself "the perfect king," "the king who is pre-eminent among kings," and "the king of justice," announcing his intention "to give justice to the people of the land, widows, and orphans, and the oppressed." Then follow about 270 lines of curses on those who dare disregard or deface his laws.[34]

The Edict of Ammisaduqa

The Edict of Ammisaduqa is not a law code but is still an important legal document. After Hammurabi, who was the sixth ruler in the Old Babylonian Dynasty, Ammisaduqa, the tenth (about 1600 B.C.), also invoked authority from Shamash (both the god of justice and the sun-god) in his inaugural edict.

This edict is unique in that it is the only substantially preserved record of the Babylonian kings' custom of proclaiming the forgiveness of debts at the beginning of their reigns and at intervals of at least seven years thereafter. Such edicts forgave all debts and obligations, returned all land holdings to their original owners, and freed all persons sold into slavery for debt. (This practice seems to be a forerunner of the Israelite law of jubilee.)

Ammisaduqa's edict listed the debts, obligations, and other releases to be granted and the penalties (usually death) for failure to comply.[35] The only women mentioned are slaves and female tavern keepers who, like merchants, are warned to give honest measure or die.

Middle Assyrian Laws

The Assyrian Dynasty rose after the breakup of the Babylonian Empire in the sixteenth century when the Hittites dethroned its dynastic rulers. The Middle Assyrian Laws were first inscribed between 1400 and 1100 B.C. The Deutsche Orientgesellschaft conducted an excavation of ancient Ashur northwest of Eshnunna on the Tigris River between 1903 and 1914. The outbreak of World War I terminated this project. Part of its discoveries were the nine tablets containing these laws. G. R. Driver and John Miles made the most important English translation in 1935.

The tablets date from the reign of Tiglath-pileser (twelfth century B.C.), but the laws themselves are believed to extend back to the fifteenth century B.C.[36] It is not known who composed them or how extensively they were used.[37] Tablets A and B (the tablets are lettered through O), are the most complete and deal with crimes, debt, corporal punishment, real property, and agriculture.

9

Tablet A deals with family relations and gives us insight into the life-and-death power of a father over his family; control of a father-in-law over his daughter-in-law in betrothal and levirate marriage; and laws affecting adultery, rape, and abortion. Tablet C, which is moderately intact, deals with slaves, rented oxen, and bailiffs. Class distinctions seem significant, but the status of these classes remains unclear due to translation difficulties.

The Hittite Code

The Hittites lived isolated from the then-known world in the mountains of eastern Turkey and did not encourage visits from travelers and merchants. The first great ruler of record was Hattusilis who consolidated the kingdom and adopted his grandson Mursilis as his successor. Mursilis proved his prowess by besieging and destroying Babylon, five hundred miles away, in about 1590 B.C. On his return to the capital at Hattusa (modern Bogaskoy), he was assassinated, and the Hittite empire remained relatively stagnant for centuries.

Hugo Winckler excavating in Bogaskoy, Anatolia, in 1906-1907 and 1911-12 unearthed some 13,000 clay tablets written front and back in cuneiform characters.[38] French scholar Frederic Hrozny deciphered the language and published a French translation in 1922. E. Neufeld published a major English translation in 1951.

These tablets contained royal decrees, treaties of Hittite monarchs, and historical, ritual, and mythological texts.[39] Many of the records are ancient indeed, but most cover the imperial age, 1400 to 1200 B.C.[40] Two of the tablets contained nearly two hundred sections of laws, though they were copies made late in the period with many sections in poor condition.

The Hittite legal code like the Middle Assyrian laws has no preamble or epilogue. Furthermore, it is attributed to no god and does not identify protection of the weak as its purpose. In this sense it is unlike earlier codes.[41] Its laws deal with murder, assault, theft, commerce, freemen, slaves, families, marriage, inheritance, and incest. They can be characterized as concise and businesslike.

A number of codes describe lawful sexual activity for men. Sex with a pig, a dog, or a sheep was punishable by death, but other animals were lawful sexual partners as was any woman not falling within the incest or adultery prohibitions. (These relationships were forbidden by penalty of death.)

Nuzi Laws and Customs

Edward Chiera, of the American School of Oriental Research in Baghdad, excavating at the ancient city of Nuzi or Nuzu in northern Iraq near modern Kirkuk in 1925-31, discovered over 4,000 clay tablets written in cuneiform script.[42] They covered four or five full generations dating from ca. 1480 to 1355 B.C. and were written in Akkadian by people who natively spoke Hurrian.[43] Chiera translated some of the Nuzi tablets into English. But the most important translation is that of E. A. Speiser of the University of Pennsylvania beginning in the late 1920s.

The Nuzi legal documents are important because they describe a number of customs with biblical parallels such as adoption for childless couples, inheritance rights of daughters, the responsibility of a wife to provide a substitute if she is unable to bear children, and benefits to slaves who bear children to their mistresses' husbands.[44]

The Law of Moses

The Mosaic law occupies a special place in Judeo-Christian culture as part of its canon. Although many codes claim a

11

divine origin, Mosaic law directly influences our current legal system. The religious-ethical tradition of the patriarchs had been lost, and there was a need for a legal system to firmly establish regulation of cultural and social mores.

The Decalogue (Ten Commandments) is ascribed to the finger of God on Mount Sinai. The text identifies Moses as the source of the codes in Exodus, Leviticus, and Deuteronomy, although most modern scholars adhere to the documentary hypothesis of Julius Wellhausen that the Pentateuch (the five books of Moses) was written by several authors between the ninth and fifth centuries B.C. The identity of the code's author is not at issue in this study.

The story of the daughters of Zelophehad (Num. 27:1-11) is an example of how the Bible claims the legal code beyond the Decalogue emerged. The issue was raised regarding the inheritance of daughters in the absence of sons. It was presented to the Lord, the God of Israel, who considered the matter, determined the result, and told Moses how to formulate a statute. In this case it was concluded if a man should die without sons, his estate would pass to his daughters and if there were no daughters to his nearest relatives (vv. 9-11).

Although many of the statutes attributable to Moses derived from specific fact situations, others may have had their origin in previous codes and nomadic customs. An example of dependence on a previous code is Exodus 21:35, which could have been copied (at least in one detail) from the Laws of Eshnunna, section 53:

> Exodus
> And if one man's ox hurt another's, that he die; then they shall sell the live ox, and divide the money of it; and the dead ox also they shall divide.

> Laws of Eshunna
> If an ox gores an(other) ox and causes (its) death, both

12

ox owners shall divide (among themselves) the price of the live ox and also the meat of the dead ox.[45]

Or compare the lex talionis (eye for an eye) provision of the Code of Hammurabi, sections 196, 197, 200, with Exodus 21:23-25; Leviticus 24:19-20; and Deuteronomy 19:21:

Code of Hammurabi
If a seignior has destroyed the eye of a member of an aristocracy, they shall destroy his eye.
If he has broken a(nother) seignior's bone, they shall break his bone.
If a seignior has knocked out a tooth of a seignior of his own rank, they shall knock out his tooth.[46]

Exodus
Thou shalt give life for life, eye for eye, tooth for tooth, hand for hand, foot for foot, burning for burning, wound for wound, stripe for stripe.

Leviticus
And if a man cause a blemish in his neighbour; as he hath one, so shall it be done to him;
Breach for breach, eye for eye, tooth for tooth: as he hath caused a blemish in a man, so shall it be done to him again.

Deuteronomy
And thine eye shall not pity; but life shall go for life, eye for eye, tooth for tooth, hand for hand, foot for foot.

A third example is this Middle Assyrian law, section 8:

If a woman has crushed a seignior's testicle in a brawl, they shall cut off one finger of hers, and if the other testicle has become affected along with it by catching the infection even though a physician has bound (it) up, or she has crushed the other testicle in the brawl, they shall tear out both her [eyes].[47]

13

Deuteronomy 24:11-12 is a striking parallel, but its stringent punishment was based on the mere act of touching a man's genitals, whether she injures him or not:

> When men strive together one with another, and the wife of the one draweth near for to deliver her husband out of the hand of him that smiteth him, and putteth forth her hand, and taketh him by the secrets: Then thou shalt cut off her hand, thine eye shall not pity her.

Although these and other similarities seem to demonstrate the natural evolution of law, the Mosaic Law was certainly unique. It set the Israelites apart yet did not leave them at an economic and legal disadvantage with their neighbors. For instance, in the matter of the ox goring described above, the Mosaic code adds the penalty of stoning the ox (Ex. 21:28); the penalty of death for the owner if he knew the ox was dangerous (v. 29); the penalty of vicarious liability if his ox gored a son or a daughter—or a payment in lieu (vv. 30-31); or the payment of damages where someone digs a pit into which an ox falls (vv. 33-34). In addition, contemporary legal systems provided multiple penalties for lawbreakers, but Israel's judges were usually limited to one penalty, generally less violent than those of their contemporaries. A major significant modification required that Hebrew slaves-for-debt be treated more as brother/servants than as slaves.

Neo-Babylonian Law

Though the most recent of these ancient codes, the Neo-Babylonian laws are the least well preserved. Only eleven sections are legible. F. E. Peiser found them in the British Museum, translated them into English, and published them in 1899. The laws date from the sixth century B.C. and cover such matters as ownership of land, the treatment of female slaves, and marriage. The most important section (12) deals with a widow's right to share in her husband's estate if he does not provide for her before his death. Nothing else is remarkably different from earlier codes.

Jewish Law

According to Jewish faith, God revealed the written law (Torah or Pentateuch) and the oral law to Moses at Sinai. Moses handed the oral law down to Joshua, where it descended to the elders of Israel, thence to the prophets (including Ezra ca. 400 B.C.), to the Great Sanhedrin, to one of the last of its eminent members, Simeon the Just (ca. 280 B.C.), and through five pairs of great scholars, ending with Hillel and Shammai. It then continued through a series of rabbis to Judah the prince, redactor of the Mishnah around A.D. 200.[48]

Ezra is usually credited with compiling the Old Testament as we have it today after Israel's return from the Babylonian exile. This means that the laws and customs of this important biblical period could have been influenced by Neo-Babylon. However, except for such stories as Daniel and Esther, there is little evidence of Neo-Babylonian law in the canon.

In 333 B. C. Jaddua, high priest at Jerusalem, surrendered on behalf of his small nation to Alexander the Great, bringing Israel under Greek domination. When Alexander's empire was divided at his death, Palestine came under the rule of the Ptolemies of Egypt until the campaign of Antiochus III in 198 B. C. moved it into the Syrian sphere of influence under the Seleucids.

In 166 B. C. the Jews, under Judas Maccabeus, revolted. After a series of victories against the Seleucid armies, Maccabean troops took over the temple mount at Jerusalem. For the next several years, control of Jerusalem swayed back and forth

15

between the Seleucids and the Maccabees.[49] Eventually, Israel became a vassal state with limited autonomy. Four groups of historical importance dominate these years of political turmoil: the Sadducees, the Pharisees, the Essenes, and the Zealots.

The Sadducees were the priestly aristocracy—the old guard—who sought to maintain the status quo. They relied on the written law and rejected the authority of oral law.[50] They were also an elite priestly family which traced its ancestry to early Israelite leaders. Through their temple administrations people's sins were forgiven (Lev. 4:20, 26). Their strategy was to maintain leadership and control of temple rites through accommodation with Seleucids, Greeks, Hasmoneans, and Romans.[51] As the position of high priest became politicized, the Sadducees lost credibility.

The Pharisees appear to have had their roots in the common people. They resisted any kind of collaboration with hellenism and made the purity of the law their rallying cry,[52] although they expanded the legal code through incorporation of oral law, which they assigned a status equal or superior to written law. They transferred worship from the temple to the home and synagogue, adapting temple purification rites as personal rites for practice at home.[53] Ironically they also borrowed hellenistic forms and forums. For example, they replaced priesthood leadership with a class of scholars and adopted logical-deductive reasoning to solve scriptural or legal problems.[54]

At some point, probably in the latter half of the second century B.C., the monastic Essenes formed in the desert, decrying the wickedness of urban Judaism, the politicizing of the temple by the Hasmoneans, and predicting divine retribution.[55] A small political group known as the Zealots also emerged. These were men of Maccabean mien who believed in political independence. In response to their revolt in A.D. 66, Roman emperor Titus destroyed Jerusalem four years later.

The Essenes buried their writings in caves near Qumran and fled down the coast of the Dead Sea to Herod's great but abandoned fortress at Massada to join the surviving Zealots, where they all perished.

Thus two of the four groups were massacred, and the third, the Sadducees, lost its basis for authority with the destruction of the temple. The Pharisees became the unchallenged spiritual leaders of Judaism.

It would be incorrect to assume a high degree of unanimity among the Pharisees on oral law. Judaism was plagued by schisms of rival schools for years.[56] Then Rabbi Judah the Prince (A.D. 170-219) sorted through the divergent opinions and reduced the oral law to writing—the Mishnah, published about A.D. 200 and accepted by virtually all significant factions. Practicing Jews accept the Torah as comprising two parts: the "Written" Torah or Old Testament and the "Oral" Torah or Mishnah.

Two major commentaries on the oral Torah then followed. The scholars of Jerusalem published the Jerusalem Talmud (Yerushalmi) in about A.D. 400. The Jewish scholars of Babylon published the Babylonian Talmud (Bavli) about A.D. 600. Both are revered, but the Babylonian Talmud is esteemed as more authoritative.

The Mishnah and the Talmud are important historical documents, created by legal scholars during the first six centuries of the Common Era. They give invaluable insights into Mosaic laws, particularly those in Leviticus and Deuteronomy. I cite them throughout the following chapters.

Notes

1. Raymond Westbrook, "Biblical and Cuneiform Law Code," *Revue Biblique* 92 (1985): 249.

2. Bernard S. Jackson, "Reflections on Biblical Criminal Law,"

Journal of Jewish Studies 24 (1973): 9.

3. Westbrook, "Biblical and Cuneiform Law," 252.

4. G. R. Driver and J. C. Miles, *The Babylonian Laws*, 2 vols. (Oxford: Oxford University Press, 1968), 1:9, 11.

5. James B. Pritchard, ed., *Ancient Near Eastern Texts* (Princeton, NJ: Princeton University Press, including Supplement, 1969), 523.

6. John Bright, *A History of Israel* (Philadelphia: Westminster Press, 1959), 35, 53.

7. Pritchard, *Ancient Near Eastern Texts*, 523.

8. Ibid.

9. Ibid.

10. Ibid., 524.

11. William W. Hallo and William K. Simpson, *The Ancient Near East, A History* (New York: Harcourt Brace Jovanovich, 1971), 80.

12. S. Langdon, "The Sumerian Law Code Compared with the Code of Hammurabi," *The Journal of the Royal Asiatic Society of Great Britain and Ireland* (1920): 491-92.

13. Pritchard, *Ancient Near Eastern Texts*, 525.

14. Langdon, "The Sumerian Law Code," 491.

15. Reuven Yaron, ed., *The Laws of Eshnunna* (Jerusalem: Magnes Press, 1969), vii.

16. Ibid., 52-55.

17. Driver and Miles, *The Babylonian Laws*, 1:9.

18. Pritchard, *Ancient Near Eastern Texts*, 159.

19. Francis Rue Steele, "The Code of Lipit-Ishtar," *American Journal of Archaeology* 51 (1947): 159; 52 (1948): 425.

20. Ibid., 52 (1948): 426-27.

21. Ibid.

22. Pritchard, *Ancient Near Eastern Texts*, 159.

23. Ibid., 161.

24. Steele, "Code of Lipit-Ishtar," 430.

25. Driver and Miles, *The Babylonian Laws*, 1:xxiv.

26. Bright, *History of Israel*, 52.

27. Driver and Miles, *The Babylonian Laws*, 1:28.

28. Pritchard, *Ancient Near Eastern Texts*, 164.

29. Code of Hammurabi 141, in Driver and Miles, *The Babylonian Laws*, 2:55.

30. Code of Hammurabi 143, in ibid., 2:57.

31. Ibid., 1:37.

32. Ibid., 1:29.

33. Ibid., 1:27-30.

34. Pritchard, *Ancient Near Eastern Texts*, 178-80.

35. Ibid., 526-28.

36. Ibid., 180; G. R. Driver and J. C. Miles, *The Assyrian Laws* (Oxford: Clarendon Press, 1935), 4-7.

37. Ibid., 12.

38. E. Neufeld, *The Hittite Laws* (London: Luzac & Co. Ltd., 1951), 70, 78.

39. Ibid., 72.

40. Ibid., 73.

41. Ibid., 101, 98.

42. Thomas L. Thompson, *The Historicity of the Patriarchal Narratives* (New York: Walter de Gruyter, 1974), 197.

43. Ibid., 199.

44. Roland de Vaux, *The Early History of Israel* (Philadelphia: Westminster Press, 1978), 241-56.

45. Pritchard, *Ancient Near Eastern Texts*, 163.

46. Ibid., 175.

47. Ibid., 181.

48. Aboth 1, 2, in Herbert Danby, trans., *The Mishnah* (Oxford: Oxford University Press, 1985), 446-49.

49. Moshe Pearlman, *The Maccabees* (Jerusalem: Weidenfeld and Nicolson, 1973), 192; J. Alberto Soggin, *A History of Israel; From the Beginnings to the Bar Kochba Revolt, A.D. 135*, trans. John Bowden (London: SCM Press Ltd., 1984), 306.

50. Solomon Zeitlin, *A Study of the History of Judaism* (New York: KTAV Publishing House, 1973), 103.

51. Soggin, *History of Israel*, 312.

52. Bright, *History of Israel*, 431.

53. Jacob Neusner, *Judaism in the Beginning of Christianity*

(Philadelphia: Fortress Press, 1984), 57.

54. Ellis Rivkin, "Pharisaism and the Crisis of the Individual in the Greco-Roman World," *Jewish Quarterly Review* 61 (July 1970): 30.

55. Neusner, *Judaism in the Beginning of Christianity*, 26.

56. George Horowitz, *The Spirit of Jewish Law* (New York: Bloch Publishing House, 1973), 32.

II.

THE LAW OF THE KEEPER

Before discussing ancient Near Eastern laws about women specifically, it may be helpful to examine family organization and the legal support system built into the nomadic lifestyle in general. This chapter describes the legal environment governing shepherds' actions and relationships and the economic and legal environment in which they lived.

Jacob's Herding Contracts

It is not difficult to deduce from Genesis that Jacob was a novice at negotiating contracts and that his uncle Laban was crafty enough to take advantage of him. Their contracts became a source of contention between them and a major issue in their confrontation in the wilderness as Jacob was fleeing back to Canaan. The whole story of Jacob's involvement with Laban, including his marriages to Rachel and Leah, is linked to his contracts with Laban. A review of herding contracts illuminates the story of Jacob and his family in Padanaram.

Old Babylonian herding contracts were drawn up once a year at shearing time, when shepherds returned the animals to their owners.[1] After shearing time a new agreement remained

21

in force until shearing time the following year. It was not un-usual for a shepherd to subcontract with shepherd boys, but he would bear responsibility to the owner for the flocks.[2]

The owner was interested in getting his flock back with the most substantial increase possible, and the shepherd was interested in keeping the reasonable expectations of the owner as low as possible and retaining part of the surplus. Two aspects of herding were critical in negotiations: the expected attrition rate and the expected birth rate. (For simplicity I have left goats and other animals out of the calculations.) The contracts reviewed are mostly Old Babylonian contracts dating from the nineteenth to sixteenth centuries B.C. and Nuzi contracts dating from the sixteenth to the fourteenth centuries B.C. According to the consensus of scholars, the terms of these contracts applied almost universally in the ancient Near East, including Canaan, during the time of the Old Testament. The contracts anticipated a 15 percent annual death rate in the herd. This would include animals dying from old age and disease.[3] To account for this natural loss, shepherds had to produce the skins complete with wool.[4]

Martha A. Morrison in her analysis of twenty-six Nuzi contracts, found the actual loss to be 17.1 percent,[5] so a rate of 15 percent would have favored the owners. Nuzi owners expected about 80 births per 100 ewes.[6] Morrison determined the actual birthrate to be 78 percent, again a little in favor of the owners. J. J. Finkelstein analyzed a number of Old Babylonian contracts and determined that an average contract would require the shepherd to guarantee the owner an increase of 66.6 sheep per 100, but the shepherd was allowed to keep anything more than that.[7] Thus if nature cooperated, both parties could be satisfied, even though the owner was the best protected. If the shepherd did not return the minimum number of animals called for in the contract, he had to replace them or obtain contractual relief to free him of the duty to replace them.

Other terms of the contract were negotiated or provided by statute. For instance the owner was expected to provide the shepherd with grain for food[8] and adequate clothing.[9] According to Morrison, shepherds were also entitled to milk and wool as part of their wages and could eat rams for meat, though of course they would account for them at the end of the contract year.[10]

Sheep could be lost through theft, attacks by wild animals, death by natural causes, acts of God, or simply by wandering off. The shepherd had to guard especially against loss from neglect. According to the Laws of Eshnunna dating from about 1900 B.C. and the Code of Hammurabi dating from about 1750 B.C., if a bailee for hire was careless or negligent, he would have to replace all missing or lost property.[11] As David Daube has pointed out, however, the Bible more leniently contains "no express provision . . . making him [the shepherd] liable in case he simply loses an animal."[12]

The cities of the Old Babylonian era were situated in the broad Tigris-Euphrates Valley. Sophisticated irrigation systems utilized the water from these great rivers to produce year-round crops. Interspersed with these productive lands were marginal lands in patchwork across the whole valley. Contract shepherds would guide their animals to these marginal areas by day and return to the sheepfolds provided by the owners by night. Therefore, the shepherds were responsible for the loss of any animals during the day, but the responsibility shifted to the owner and his sheepfold by night.[13] In this instance the fold was a fenced enclosure with a gate and sometimes a watchtower provided by the owner or his agent.[14]

Attacks by wild beasts were a major concern for shepherds. The general rule was that the shepherd had a reasonable responsibility to safeguard the flock but not at the risk of his own life. If the attacking beast was one that could threaten his life—a bear or a lion—he was only required to attempt to recover pieces of the slain animal as evidence that it had been consumed by a predator.[15] Similarly if the animals were killed by lightning, floods, or accidents which a man could not reasonably defend against, the shepherd would not have to replace them.[16]

What if a sheep or lamb wandered off? There is no provision in the Old Testament that would make a shepherd liable for replacing a sheep lost in this way.[17] We can assume that if a shepherd could show a reasonable standard of care, he would not have to replace lost sheep. If he was proved negligent, he would have to replace them.[18]

How does all this apply to the narrative of Jacob? Jacob's first contract with Laban was to care for his flock for seven years to pay the bride-price for Rachel's hand in marriage. We know nothing more about this contract. Similarly the second contract for another seven years' service for Rachel's hand—the first seven years having arbitrarily become the bride-price for Leah—did not contain any other terms of which we are aware. Any blanks in these two simple oral agreements would be filled in by the laws and customs discussed above.

Jacob and Laban negotiated a third contract when Jacob told Laban that he wanted to return to Canaan. Laban was anxious to dissuade Jacob from leaving and said, "For I have learned by experience that the Lord hath blessed me for thy sake" (Gen. 30:27). However, after fourteen years under Laban's domination, Jacob was no longer a novice negotiator. Jacob had learned how to produce a multi-colored flock—a rarity among Near Eastern flocks today and from the context of the narrative also a rarity in Laban's day.

So Jacob contracted with Laban to keep the flocks in exchange for "the speckled and spotted cattle, and all the brown . . . sheep, and the spotted and speckled among the goats" (Gen. 31:32). Further Jacob stated that any solid-colored animals in his possession should be considered stolen and therefore subject to a replacement penalty of at least twofold (v. 33). Laban readily agreed to this contract, for in a normal situation this contract would cost him no more than a couple of animals per hundred and not the 10-20 per hundred that most contracts called for.

Jacob removed his little flock of colored, spotted, speckled, and ringstraked sheep and goats three days' distance from Laban's flocks so there could be no chance of intermingling. Then Jacob did a curious thing. He took poles of green poplar, hazel, and chestnut and hacked, slashed, and partially stripped them until they looked multicolored. He planted these all around the troughs or watering holes with the intention that the animals would see them while breeding and impart these attributes to their offspring.

Ancient Near East folklore held that thoughts during conjugal relations or experiences during pregnancy affected the nature and characteristics of the child. Even the Shulhan Arukh, a sixteenth-century A.D. Jewish codification, recommended that a couple think on the Torah during sexual intercourse so that the child conceived would love the Torah.[19] Whatever the scientific merits of Jacob's theory, "the flocks conceived before the rods, and brought forth cattle ringstraked, speckled, and spotted" (Gen. 30:39).

For at least six years Jacob served Laban under their third recorded contract, making at least twenty years of service in all (Gen. 31:38, 41).[20] Jacob became wealthy under their new arrangement, and Laban saw his flocks and herds dwindle. "And Jacob beheld the countenance of Laban, and behold, it was not toward him as before" (v. 2). The Lord visited Jacob and told him to return to the land of his fathers and that he would protect him (v. 3).

Jacob's contract was fulfilled at the time of shearing, so he did not violate his contract by leaving.[21] When Laban was away shearing his own flocks, Jacob left for Canaan. Angry at this surprise departure, Laban tracked down Jacob for a confrontation. Jacob defended himself with equal vigor:

> And Jacob was wroth, and chode with Laban . . . .
> This twenty years have I been with thee; thy ewes and thy she goats have not cast {aborted} their young, and the rams of thy flock have I not eaten.
> That which was torn of beasts I brought not unto thee; I bare the loss of it; of my hand didst thou require it, whether stolen by day, or stolen by night.
> Thus I was; in the day the drought consumed me, and the frost by night; and my sleep departed from mine eyes (Gen. 31:36-40).

Jacob further complained that Laban had changed his wages ten times (contracts were renewed after every shearing season), and Laban did not refute the charge (Gen. 31:41). So it seems that Laban unilaterally changed whatever percentage of animals was to belong to Jacob, and the quantity of food, raiment, or other compensation, the details of which are not given. Laban did not challenge any of Jacob's charges, indicating that he had in fact violated every known custom or law governing shepherds for hire.

Laban recommended that they enter into one last contract: that they would never again come against each other in anger and that Jacob would not add to nor mistreat his wives (Gen. 31:44-53).

It appears that in all their contractual relationships, Jacob exceeded his obligations and was more faithful than a shepherd was reasonably expected to be. In contrast Laban's demands and expectations exuded greed.

The Sale of Joseph into Egypt

It was no secret that Joseph's brothers despised him. He was Jacob's favorite son. His troubles may have begun when he informed on some of his brothers (Gen. 37:2). Later he had two dreams, in which his brothers and parents bowed down to him (vv. 5-10). Even his father was upset by the dreams.

Jacob gave Joseph an expensive "coat," which further alienated his brothers, for it seems to have symbolized a position of superior rank. (One scholar, Emanuel Feldman, claims that it represented priesthood authority over his brothers and was similar to the special cloaks provided the high priests in the future temple in Israel.[22])

One day when the family was living near Hebron, Jacob called Joseph to him. His brothers were tending the flocks, working their way north with the receding spring rains. Jacob thought that they would be near Shechem by now and asked Joseph to check on them. Joseph complied, but arriving near Shechem, he could not find his brothers and the flocks. From a field worker, Joseph learned that his brothers were farther north. He found them in a field near Dothan about twelve miles away.

Recognizing his coat from a distance, his brothers conspired to kill him. "Come now therefore, and let us slay him, and cast him into some pit, and we will say, Some evil beast hath devoured him: and we shall see what will become of his dreams" (Gen. 37:20).

Reuben, the firstborn, persuaded them to modify this plan: "And Reuben . . . said unto them, Shed no blood, but cast him into this pit that is in the wilderness, and lay no hand upon him; [saying this] that he might rid him out of their hands, to deliver him to his father again" (Gen. 37:21-22).

What were Reuben's motives? David Daube argues that the responsibilities of the firstborn son toward his siblings included the same duties and responsibilities as those of a shepherd or bailee for hire.[23] Certainly it is well established that the firstborn had serious familial responsibilities. While his father was alive, and under his direction, the firstborn was responsible for the flocks and herds of the family. After his father's death the firstborn son was responsible for the support of his mother and sisters. He had to provide his sisters with a dowry and arrange for their marriages. If one of his brothers or sisters was murdered, he was responsible for finding the perpetrator and avenging his sibling's death.

In support of Daube's argument, it seems that Jacob's firstborn son did recognize a responsibility to protect his siblings. For example, many years later when Reuben was trying to convince Jacob to let him take Benjamin to Egypt to prove that he and his brothers were not spies, Reuben said to his father: "Slay my two sons, if I bring him [Benjamin] not to thee: deliver him into my hand, and I will bring him to thee again" (Gen. 42:30, 37).

In Dothan the brothers spied a merchant caravan of Ishmaelites. Judah suggested they sell Joseph to them as a slave. Kidnapping and selling your brother was a capital offense under Old Babylonian law.[24]

Reuben faltered as a leader here and appeared to go along with the plan, though he had planned to release Joseph. The Bible records that "his brethren were content {with Judah's suggestion}" (Gen. 37:27).

Meanwhile Joseph was probably not aware that his brothers had intended to kill him. Indignant at his treatment, he must have made a lot of noise, for a band of Midianite merchantmen heard him, got to the pit first, "rescued" him, and sold him for twenty pieces of silver to Ishmaelite traders on their way to Egypt (Gen. 37:28).

When Reuben approached the pit alone intending to release Joseph before the rest carried out their design to sell him, he found it empty. Shocked and afraid, Reuben "rent his clothes" (Gen. 37:29) and then raced back to his brethren, crying, "The child is not; and *I*, whither shall *I* go?" (v. 30, italics added).

This phrasing suggests that his concern for Joseph was not founded in love for the boy but in the firstborn's responsibility. He was concerned for himself and his future as family leader.

Joseph had joined the world of slavery, and his brothers were about to enact a cover-up drawn from the laws and customs of the keeper or shepherd. As shepherds the brothers decided upon a solution that would exonerate Reuben. They took Joseph's coat and tore it as if it had been ripped by wild beasts. According to the Code of Hammurabi, when a wild beast destroyed an animal from the flock, the owner was entitled to the remnants that could be recovered.[25] The brothers killed a kid, dipped the shredded coat in its blood, and took it back to Jacob as evidence that Joseph had been slain by wild beasts. They pressed him for a judgment: "This have we found: know now whether it be thy son's coat or no" (Gen. 37:32).

This question supports the contention that Reuben and his brothers were attempting to avoid legal obligation.[26] Jacob had to accept the irrefutable evidence. He acknowledged: "It is my son's coat; an evil beast hath devoured him; Joseph is without doubt rent in pieces" (Gen. 37:32-33). Reuben and his brothers were free of any further responsibility for Joseph.

Daube suggests that Jacob despite his acknowledgement either had or developed doubts about Joseph's death.[27] Many years later when Judah explains the family history to the Egyptian official who is in reality his younger brother, he quotes his father as saying, "And the one [Joseph] went out from me, and I said, surely he is torn in pieces; and I saw him not since." Why would Jacob say "and I said"? Daube claims he had to say it as a legal requirement, having been formally asked to "discern" the evidence of the torn and bloody robe. Daube also reads Jacob's statement, "and I saw him not since," as Jacob's opinion that his son was absent, not dead. Thus Jacob made these statements when the evidence was presented to him because it was formally required—not necessarily because he believed it. He refused to let his sons take Benjamin to Egypt with them because he still neither trusted nor believed them. He would not even accept Reuben's death oath regarding his sons as sufficient surety to let Benjamin go (Gen. 42:37). It was not until they were again starving and Judah asserted his leadership and also agreed to stand as surety for Benjamin that Jacob finally relented and let them go.

When Judah and his brothers presented themselves before Joseph, Benjamin was with them. Joseph, who had not seen Benjamin, his only full brother, in about twenty-two years,[28] was overcome with emotion and had to leave the audience chamber to regain his control (Gen. 43:30). Upon returning he hosted a meal with his brothers, arranging them at their table in order of their family seniority. The brothers wondered at this and also at the fact that he had five times as much food presented to Benjamin than to any of the other brothers.

After he had completed a sale of grain, Joseph instructed his servants to return their money to his brother's sacks and to hide his special silver divining cup in Benjamin's sack (Gen. 44:2, 5).[29]

When they had traveled but a short distance from the city, Joseph sent his servants after them to accuse them of stealing his divining cup. Of course the brothers protested their innocence and said, "With whomsoever of thy servants it be found, both let him die, and we also will be my lord's bondmen" (Gen. 44:9). This was nothing more than a statement of the Code of Hammurabi regarding the theft of sacred things.[30]

When the chalice was found, the men were devastated. When presented to Joseph, they all prostrated themselves at his feet. "What deed is this that ye have done? wot ye not that such a man as I can certainly divine?" (Gen. 44:15), Joseph asked. He then said he would keep Benjamin and the others could go. Judah took the lead at this moment, offering himself in exchange for Benjamin (vv. 16-34).

30

Judah, unquestionably a villain in the first part of the story, thus becomes the hero in the second part. According to Maimonides, a twelfth-century A.D. Jewish scholar, one cannot know if he has overcome temptation until he finds himself in the same circumstances as when he first sinned. If he resists the second time, his repentance is complete.[31]

David Chinitz hypothesizes that this belief motivated Joseph to create the complicated charade he played on his brothers.[32] Whatever his motivation his charade allowed all his brethren to show that they had considerable remorse for their involvement in his demise. Perhaps as a result of Judah's honorable conduct, he later received the firstborn blessing of Jacob giving him leadership over Israel (Gen. 49:10; 1 Chr. 5:1-2).

David the Shepherd

David was the most famous shepherd of the western world. During his legendary confrontation with Goliath, David had been tending the family flocks. The prophet Samuel had already anointed him next king of Israel (1 Sam. 16:13).

David arrived at Saul's camp with food for his brothers, who were serving as soldiers. Goliath took his customary position in the valley and issued his usual challenge. David was incensed at this "uncircumcised Philistine" (1 Sam. 17:26) and was talking with some soldiers when his brother Eliab spotted him. Fearing that David had left the flocks at home unguarded—a responsibility that Eliab as firstborn had assigned David—Eliab became angry. He said, "And with whom hast thou left those few sheep in the wilderness?" (v. 28). David gave a classic younger brother response: "What have I now done?" (v. 29). Eliab had every right to be concerned, for the flock was his responsibility as the firstborn. As a matter of fact, David had left them with a keeper (v. 20).

31

Incensed by Goliath's challenge, David went to Saul offering to challenge the giant. Saul was swayed when David told him, "Thy servant kept his father's sheep, and there came a lion, and a bear, and took a lamb out of the flock; And I went out after him and smote him, and delivered it out of his mouth: and when he arose against me, I caught him by his beard, and smote him, and slew him" (1 Sam. 17:34-35).

It is not clear whether David was talking about one occasion or two, since bears and lions do not act in concert. In any event Saul knew that it was remarkable for a shepherd to stand against such odds when there was no legal or moral obligation, and that it required skill as well as courage. The rest of the story is well known: David slew the Philistine.

Cain and Abel

In Genesis 4 appears an account of the first recorded murder, which also illuminates aspects of the law of the keeper.

Cain was a tiller of the soil while Abel made his living keeping flocks. On a certain day both brought offerings to the altar. According to the narrative, Cain "brought of the fruit of the ground an offering unto the Lord," while Abel "brought of the firstlings of his flock and of the fat thereof" (Gen. 4:3-4).

Abel's offering is described as acceptable by the terms "firstlings" and "fat," while no qualifiers modify Cain's offering, which God rejected. Incensed and vengeful, Cain sought his brother and his flocks, killed Abel, and then buried him to hide the evidence. A short while later, the Lord God asked Cain, "Where is Abel thy brother?" Cain answered, "I know not: Am I my brother's keeper?" (Gen. 4:9).

Acccording to Middle Eastern law, Cain, as the elder son, possibly the firstborn, *was* his brother's keeper. Although this story, by its metaphor, may reveal more about the time when it was written than anything else, we see the pervasiveness of law in biblical narrative and its importance in family relationships.

Notes

1. J. N. Postgate, "Some Old Babylonian Shepherds and Their Flocks," *Journal of Semitic Studies* 20 (1975): 2.

2. J. J. Finkelstein, "An Old Babylonian Herding Contract and Gen. 31:38f," *Journal of Ancient Oriental Studies* 88 (1968): 31.

3. Postgate, "Babylonian Shepherds and Their Flocks," 6.

4. Ibid.

5. Martha A. Morrison, "Evidence for Herdsmen and Animal Husbandry in Nuzi Documents," in *Studies on the Civilization and Culture of Nuzi and the Hurrians, in Honor of Ernest R. Lacheman*, eds. M. A. Morrison and D. I. Owen (Winona Lake, IN: Eisenbrauns, 1981), 282.

6. Martha A. Morrison, "The Jacob and Laban Narrative in Light of Near Eastern Sources," *The Biblical Archeologist* 46 (Summer 1983): 156.

7. Finkelstein, "Old Babylonian Herding Contract," 34.

8. Postgate, "Babylonian Shepherds and Their Flocks," 9.

9. Finkelstein, "Old Babylonian Herding Contract," 36.

10. Morrison, "The Jacob and Laban Narrative," 156-57.

11. Law of Eshnunna 5, in Reuven Yaron, *The Laws of Eshnunna* (Jerusalem: The Magnes Press, 1969), 23; Code of Hammurabi 125, in G. R. Driver and J. C. Miles, *The Babylonian Laws*, 2 vols. (Oxford: Oxford University Press, 1968), 2:51.

12. David Daube, "Negligence in the Early Talmudic Law of Contract," in *Festschrift Fritz Schulz* (Weimar: Hermann Bohlaus Nachfolger, 1951), 145.

13. Driver and Miles, *The Babylonian Laws*, 1:460.

14. Ibid.

15. "If a visitation of god has occurred in a sheepfold or a lion has made a kill, the shepherd shall prove himself innocent in the presence of god, but the owner or the sheepfold shall receive from him the animal stricken in the fold." Code of Hammurabi 266, in

James B. Pritchard, ed., *Ancient Near Eastern Texts* (Princeton, NJ: Princeton University Press, including Supplement, 1969), 177; Sumerian Law 9, in ibid., 526; Ex. 22:13; Amos 3:12.

16. Baba Mezia 93b, in Soncino. I. Epstein, ed. and trans., *The Babylonian Talmud* (London: The Soncino Press, 1948), 540-41.

17. Daube, "Negligence in Early Talmudic Law," 145.

18. Finkelstein, "Old Babylonian Herding Contract," 31.

19. Rabbi Solomon Ganzfried, *Code of Jewish Law: Kitzen Shulhan Arukh*, trans. Hyman E. Goldin (New York: Hebrew Publishing Company, 1963), 4.14 [150:2]. This tradition endures even today. When I was living in the village of Abu Dis on the West Bank and visiting the home of an Arab family in 1977, I was introduced to all the sons, six handsome dark-haired young men. Then a girl of about twelve with flaming red hair came into the room. She was their sister. How did she come to have such beautiful red hair when everyone else in the family had dark hair? I was told that while her mother was pregnant, she rode the bus into Jerusalem and while disembarking saw a European woman with flaming red hair—and that was why the daughter was born with the same beautiful hair.

20. Clarke speculates that it might have been closer to forty based on a consideration of the ages of the children upon their arrival at Shechem. Adam Clarke, *The Holy Bible Containing the Old and New Testaments with a Commentary and Critical Notes* (1830; rprt., Nashville, TN: Abingdon Press, n.d.), 1:197-99.

21. Morrison, "Jacob and Laban Narrative," 158.

22. Emanuel Feldman, "Joseph and the Biblical Echo," *Dor le Dor* 13 (1985): 162.

23. David Daube, *Studies in Biblical Law* (New York: KTAV Publishing House, 1969), 4.

24. Code of Hammurabi 14, in Driver and Miles, *The Babylonian Laws*, 2:19.

25. Code of Hammurabi 266, in Pritchard, *Ancient Near Eastern Texts*, 177.

26. See Daube, *Studies in Biblical Law*, 6.

27. Ibid., 9.

THE LAW OF THE KEEPER

28. Stuart A. West, "Judah and Tamar—A Scriptural Enigma," *Dor le Dor* 12 (1984): 246n2.

29. R. L. Harris, G. L. Archer Jr., and B. K. Waltke, eds., *Theological Wordbook of the Old Testament* (Chicago: Moody Press, 1980), 2:572.

30. "If a man has stolen property belonging to a god or a palace, that man shall be put to death, and he who has received the stolen property from his hand shall be put to death." Code of Hammurabi 6, in Driver and Miles, *The Babylonian Laws*, 2:15; see also Gen. 31:32, the tale of Rachel's stealing Laban's household images.

31. David Chinitz, "Joseph and His Brothers," *Dor le Dor* 14 (1986): 183.

32. Ibid.

III.

RACHEL'S HOUSEHOLD

The story of Rachel's household provides a useful place to begin exploring the legal issues of the Bible which relate to the status of women. Many of the legal issues common to the other narratives are focused in this story.

Rachel

According to Josephus, Rachel's "beauty . . . was so flourishing, as few of the women of that age could vie with."[1] If so, perhaps her beauty was a snare, for her father used it to his advantage and her suitor seemed blinded by it.

Rachel and her elder sister Leah seem to have been the oldest children of Laban, for Rachel first appears in the narrative attending the flocks of her father. If there had been sons of age, they probably would have attended the flocks. She must have been at least eleven years old, for rarely would flocks be entrusted to a younger person.

We are introduced to her at the well of Haran—the same well where Rebekah met the servant of Abraham and shortly thereafter became betrothed to Isaac. Here then is a clue to the ensuing story, for whenever a maiden meets a young man at a well in the biblical narratives, marriage is a result.[2] As Rachel led her flocks to water that evening, she was greeted by a commotion at the well. Several of her peers ran to her excitedly, telling her a stranger at the well had come to seek her father.

Rachel came to him and asked, "Who are you, sir; whence have you come; and why do you seek my father?"[3]

Jacob responded, "If you are truly the daughter of Laban, we are related. For Terah had three sons—Abraham, Haran, and Nahor. Nahor had a son Bethuel, who is your [grand]father. Bethuel also had a daughter, Rebekah, who is my mother and my father is Isaac, son of Abraham. I am Jacob, and we are cross-cousins."[4]

At the mention of her aunt's name, Rachel began to weep, for Rebecca was often mentioned by her brother. She was so happy and excited she willingly allowed Jacob to embrace and kiss her. "Come, come," she cried. "My father will be so excited to see you. He speaks so often of your mother and has longed to hear of her. Come quickly."

"I am most anxious to meet your father, but first let's water your flocks. Then we can visit uninterrupted."

"But it is not time. It is a community well, and we do not water the flocks until all are here and together roll away the stone."

"Tonight, I will roll away the stone and water your flocks."

Rachel suppressed a protest and marvelled at the strength of Jacob as he rolled away the great stone covering the well.

When he had finished watering the flock, Rachel, hurrying ahead, led him home. "Father, father," she cried as they approached. "Jacob has come. Jacob, the son of Rebekah. Come, quickly."

Laban came from the house and greeted Jacob warmly with a phrase reflecting recognition of kinship: "Surely thou art my bone and my flesh."[5]

Rachel was interested in her cousin and was aware of his

interest in her. Her father also became aware of this interest. The ancient world found kinship a sound economic and social basis for marriage, and Laban recognized Jacob as a worthy spouse by that measure. Perhaps he also felt that Jacob would be a useful shepherd for his flocks.

After a month Rachel's father invited Jacob to sit with him in something more than a friendly chat. It was a formal invitation to negotiate a contract for Jacob's services which, I believe, Laban intended to use as a pretext for a betrothal agreement for Rachel. The principals in a marriage contract were the bride and the groom. The contract—the provisions apply generally to all marriage contracts from the old Babylonian period down to and including Jewish law—was typically written by the bride's father or legal guardian such as the firstborn son who had inherited this responsibility from a deceased father. Either the groom or the groom's agent, usually his father or another relative, would open negotiations with the bride's father or guardian. Once they reached an agreement, they drafted a document and/or called witnesses to whom they revealed the details of the contract.

Few marriage contracts would have been as informal as the brief mention given in Genesis. Agreements included various clauses: the amount of the woman's dowry, that it would be returned to her along with any other penalty in the event of a divorce, the responsibility of support, the prohibition of the husband from taking other wives, and the taking of a sister or slave as a second wife.

Written marriage contracts were required under some codes as early as the first half of the second millennium B.C. Section 128 of the Code of Hammurabi, for example, invalidated any marital relationship without a written document. Oral contracts were recognized under Hittite law and in Israel for centuries after Hammurabi, although such contracts were only as good as the memory of the witnesses. Nevertheless, informal marriage was recognized in Israel as long as it met two legal conditions: intent and consummation. If a man and woman intended to act toward each other as husband and wife and raise a family and consummated these intentions, they were deemed to be legally married.

It was no surprise to Rachel when her father negotiated a contract in which Jacob would contribute seven years labor as a shepherd in payment of a bride-price for Rachel. The origins of the bride-price are unknown. It was negotiated between the suitor and the prospective bride's father or legal guardian. Some scholars believe that the bride-price in a sense purchased the wife and that she thereby became chattel or possession of her husband.[6] However, no ancient legal code contains statutes suggesting that wives were regarded as chattels.[7] Generally, the bride's father included the bride-price in her dowry.

Another thesis is that the bride-price compensated a woman for the loss of her virginity. This notion may have some validity, since non-virgins commanded lower bride-prices. The average bride-price under Jewish law from the times of Moses to the days of the Talmud was fifty shekels or 200 *zuzim*,[8] enough money to keep a woman clothed for a year with four dresses, a standard still used in Arab cultures. The two hundred *zuzim* may equal the biblical fifty shekels of silver, the amount given as the price of virginity (Deut. 22:29). The four dresses symbolized the husband's ongoing responsibility to provide his wife with clothes.[9] The average bride-price of a non-virgin was fifty *zuzim*. However, because the bride-price was technically paid to the bride's father, it would actually compensate him for having protected her virginity, not her directly. The stigma of a lesser bride-price may very well have been an incentive for the men of a household to protect their daughters or sisters against mistreatment. But I cannot see any other direct correlation between bride-price and virginity.

In reality, the bride-price seems to have originated as

compensation to a father's household for a daughter's lost services or a husband's symbolic purchase of those services.[10] The bride-price also provided legal consideration for the marriage contract, and it gave the groom an opportunity to display his ability to support his new bride. In Jacob's case the actual bride-price may have included more than just his labor for hire. Laban seems to have neglected providing his daughters with dowries. The only hint of a dowry is Laban's gift of Zilpah and Bilhah to his daughters. When Jacob talked with Rachel and Leah about moving to his homeland in Canaan, they expressed hostile feelings toward their father, "Are we not counted of him strangers? for he hath sold us, and hath quite devoured also our money" (see Gen. 31:15).

What money do they mean, since no money apparently changed hands? Either Jacob paid cash in addition to his services or the sisters computed the average bride-price as (for the sake of argument) thirty shekels of silver while Jacob had paid (again for the sake of argument) at least seventy. The slaves, Zilpah and Bilhah, were probably valued from a low of fifteen shekels of silver to a high of thirty shekels each. Thus Jacob's wives may have felt that their father had cheated them of part of their expected marital security.

A bride-price did not necessarily take the form of a lump-sum payment. It was not uncommon to pay the bride-price over time. Rachel must have been pleased for the bride-price was huge by contemporary standards.[11] Upon payment and acceptance of the bride-price, the couple was officially betrothed.

For seven years Rachel and Jacob prepared for the event. Tents were woven of goathair, dresses and robes were made, utensils collected. When the seven years were ended, Jacob went to the house of Rachel's father to remind him of the contract. Laban called for the wedding feast, and messages were sent throughout the country for family and friends to gather.

The celebration lasted all the first day and long into the night. Rachel left the ceremony to go to the wedding tent. On the way, she was probably kidnapped and secreted away where she could not interfere with her father's plans. By agreement with Laban Leah went into the wedding tent and entered the nuptial bed. When Jacob entered the tent a little later in the dark and probably a little inebriated from the day-long celebration, he consummated his contract with a silent partner. Another grieved elsewhere.

In the light of early morning, Jacob was startled to find Leah in the bed. No doubt Jacob challenged her, "What are you doing here?"

No doubt Leah directed any blame toward her father, "My father made me do it."

Whereupon Jacob leaped from the tent and ran to Laban. "What is this thou hast done unto me? did not I serve with thee for Rachel? wherefore then hast thou beguiled me?" (Gen. 29:25).

Laban's response was deceptive. "It must not be so done in our country, to give the younger before the firstborn," he said and then offered him Rachel on the same terms but without a waiting period if he would keep Leah (Gen. 29:26-27).

Laban's response must have infuriated Jacob even more. First of all, Laban's claim that such a marriage went against the custom of the land was false—there was no such custom or Jacob and Rachel would have known of it. Jacob had never had any intent to enter into a marriage with Leah.

Jacob could have had the marriage annulled, but there were no tribunals to which Jacob could resort. Jacob was in Laban's domain without independent means and unable to return to his own land for fear of his brother. His recourse was limited. A patriarchal potentate had created a case-specific law: Jacob could have Rachel along with Leah or not at all. Jacob opted to have Rachel on Laban's terms and honored his marriage to Leah. He agreed to Laban's stipulation under duress and thus, at the end of Leah's marital week, Jacob married Rachel.[12]

Laban presented each of his daughters with a handmaid for a dowry—Bilhah to Rachel and Zilpah to Leah. The most important legal consideration in a marital contract was the dowry, the property the bride brought to the husband upon marriage or wedding gifts to the couple from her parents. The dowry, which usually far exceeded the bride-price, was a wife's opportunity to inherit from her father. It created stability in her new relationship and gave the new couple a significant economic start.[13]

Fathers could gift land to their daughters and daughters could own land, but generally sons inherited real property and related chattels. As a matter of honor, a father tried to provide for the well-being of his daughters. Tradition dictated that the dowry amount to about one-tenth of her father's estate.

The wife held legal title to her dowry property, even though the husband generally controlled and managed it.[14] If the marriage was dissolved, most legal systems required that the dowry be returned whole. Some laws added additional penalties.[15] During the marriage, such property could be sold only with the wife's consent.[16] If, during the husband's stewardship, the property was diminished or wasted, he would have to make it whole. This strong economic deterrent to divorce lent stability to the marriage relationship. As a result the dowry was usually substantial—not enough to give a couple financial independence but enough to provide the couple with help at the beginning of the marriage, to guarantee the wife a minimum standard of living, and to discourage divorce.[17]

Because the handmaids were dowry for Laban's daughters, the handmaids were the property of Jacob's wives, under his management. Laban's deceit and renegotiated proposition forced Jacob into a polygynous marriage. Although Rachel must have been upset by this situation, Jacob did not demur. Apparently there was nothing objectionable to the system. But Jacob quite clearly did not like the terms he had been forced to make. The ease with which Jacob accepted polygynous marriage would suggest that it was common in his day. But this was not so. It was an option but not an expectation. While two-wife marriages can be found in old Babylonian contracts, the practice does not appear to be common.

Many women in the Bible, including Sarah, Rachel, and Bathsheba, lived in polygyny in contrast to women in neighboring communities. There is evidence that the practice may have been widespread among Israel at times.[18] For instance we are told that in the wilderness Israel had 603,550 soldiers over the age of twenty. Of this number 22,273 were firstborn males making twenty-seven male children per family.[19] Only polygynous marriages could produce such large numbers.

Any wife who had a contract manifesting intent, a bride-price and dowry, and consummation was designated a chief wife.[20] At the time of the patriarchs, laws generally recognized five categories of childbearing women legally attached to a man: chief wife, concubine, captive wife, slave wife, and slave female. Social classes for men also ranged from patriarch to slave.

The patriarch was the legal head of the family and the chief wife or matriarch the legal head of the household responsible for all subwives, concubines, female slaves, and any or all children (Gen. 30:16). The patriarch and chief wife lived together, and a plural wife had to pursue her legal right to have children through the chief wife (v. 15). The chief wife, queen wife, primary wife, or matriarch had a legal right to be supported by any and all children, especially the firstborn, at the same level as during the patriarch's lifetime.

In a polygynous marriage more than one woman might be a chief wife, but only one woman, the first chronological wife, would be the chief wife. Both Rachel and Leah were chief wives.

Laban and Jacob negotiated a contract for each; for each, consideration was paid (bride-price) and received (dowry). Both unions were consummated. Chronologically Leah was the first wife. But Jacob's intent was that Rachel should be his first (and only) wife. He became Leah's husband only through fraud. Technically Jacob did not affirm his marriage to Leah until after his contract for Rachel was reaffirmed. So Rachel's contract remained the first contract and Leah's second. Thus Rachel was recognized as *the* chief wife (Gen. 30:15); Leah was *a* chief wife.

In quick succession Leah bore four sons: Reuben, Simeon, Levi, and Judah. Meanwhile Rachel was beside herself with grief. She could not become pregnant and desperately wanted a child. Women had a legal right to demand that their husbands do everything in their power to father children. Rachel seemed to have this in mind when she demanded of Jacob, "Give me children, or else I die" (Gen. 30:1). Rebuked by Jacob for suggesting it was his fault, she said, "Behold my maid Bilhah, go in unto her; and she shall bear upon my knees, that I may also have children by her" (v. 3). "Upon my knees" is a phrase through which Rachel invoked a legal fiction: any child borne by Bilhah in marriage to Jacob could be claimed as her own. Bilhah bore a son whom Rachel named Dan ("he has judged or vindicated") and then another whom Rachel named Naphtali ("my wrestling—the wrestlings of God have I wrestled with my sister"; see vv. 6-8).

Rachel's presentation of her handmaid, Bilhah, to Jacob in marriage is covered by precedent. A barren chief wife may present her personal slave to her husband for impregnation. The resulting child or children are legally the chief wife's, although she may choose to delay the decision. Sarah and Rachel did.

In the case of Leah's slave Zilpah, however, we have a marriage that did not conform to any ancient legal provision

45

that we know about. Generally the laws of Hammurabi and other systems promoted monogamy except in the case of a barren or sickly wife.[21] Perhaps the precedent for Leah's action originated in nomadic custom or patriarchal tradition and was not included in a written code. Or perhaps Leah was thought to be incapable of having more children.

The Code of Hammurabi does speak of cases where both the chief wife and a slave-wife or concubine bore children,[22] but we do not know the facts of those cases. Perhaps the chief wife became pregnant after presenting her handmaid to her husband as in the case of Rachel. Nahor, Abram's brother and a patriarch, had eight children by his wife Milcah and four children by his concubine Reumah (Gen. 22:20-24), but again we do not know who bore children first.

As the episode with the mandrakes shows, Rachel as chief wife could regulate the connubial rights of Leah and through her the slave-wife Zilpah. However, Leah as a chief wife had connubial rights which neither Rachel nor Jacob could deny.

Apparently it was after the births of all of Leah's sons that Rachel gave birth to Joseph (see Gen. 30:24) and then died giving birth to her second son, Benjamin (see 35:18). In death Rachel gave her sister Leah the gift she would not give her in life. After Rachel's death Leah no longer had competition for the position of *the* chief wife.

Leah

Leah seems at best to have been unhappy. She appears to have been Laban's firstborn child, but she stood constantly in the shadow of her younger sister's beauty and charm. It was not until after Rachel's death that Leah rose to primacy in marriage. But she did achieve a primacy in her own right through her sons.

Leah first comes to prominence at the wedding feast for

her sister Rachel and Jacob. Somehow Laban must have convinced her it was not only proper but her right as the elder sister to supplant Rachel in the marriage bed. Laban may have rigged this situation, not only to get Jacob's continued services but also to dispose of his obligations to Leah. All legal codes dealing with the subject give an unmarried daughter claim on her father for maintenance throughout her life. A childless woman, whether widowed or divorced, always had the right to return to her paternal estate for support even after her father's death. The father's heirs inherited the responsibility to provide for her if necessary. During marriage a husband was responsible for his wife's maintenance, dowry notwithstanding. A son was responsible for the support of his widowed mother—the firstborn son in Hebrew law and all sons equally under most other legal systems.[23]

Leah's narrative is one of few involving female-initiated fornication. She knowingly impersonated her sister—or at least allowed Jacob to assume that she was her sister—and consummated the marriage that had been solemnized between Rachel and Jacob. Mosaic law does not cover the case of a single woman seducing a man except in the special case of a priest's daughter for "playing the whore." In this case she would be "burnt with fire" (Lev. 21:9). It was not legally possible for a single woman to commit "adultery." Thus the encounter between unmarried Leah and married Jacob would not be deemed adulterous.[24]

The narrative of Jacob and Leah does not hint at a penalty for fornication. Middle Assyrian, Hittite, Mosaic, and Jewish law are the only legal systems that address this issue and then only from the lawmaker's (male) viewpoint. The Hittite code merely says that if a man cohabits with a free woman, slave-girl, or harlot, there is no punishment.[25]

Middle Assyrian law draws an important distinction between rape and seduction—a distinction which is lost in Mosaic and Jewish law. If a man rapes a virgin, his wife is punished.[26] However, if he seduces the virgin (she consents to relations), his wife cannot be touched and the man is fined one-third of the "value of a virgin."[27]

Mosaic law is less clear. According to Exodus 22:16: "And if a man entice {seduce} a maid that is not betrothed, and lie with her, he shall surely endow her to be his wife. If her father utterly refuse to give her unto him, he shall pay money according to the dowry of virgins." In Deuteronomy 22:28-29: "If a man find a damsel that is a virgin, which is not betrothed, and lay hold on (seize) her, and lie with her, and they be found; Then the man that lay with her shall give unto the damsel's father fifty shekels of silver, and she shall be his wife; because he hath humbled her, he may not put her away all his days." In the first case the maiden consents to the seduction or fornication, and in the second case she is raped. In both instances the penalties are the same. The male has to pay the dowry of virgins (fifty shekels) and marry the woman. Jewish law follows these two cases and holds that both rape and seduction represent theft of virginity for which the penalties are a fine and marriage.[28]

If the sexual offenses of seduction and rape merge in the case of the male, then perhaps the same is true of the female. Just as there is no such crime as female rape of a man, then perhaps there is no such crime as female seduction of a male. Leah's action may have been morally reprehensible, but she committed no crime or tort.

At worst then Leah was simply no longer a virgin. Her father could no longer negotiate with a prospective husband for the "dowry of virgins" (Ex. 22:17). Leah's bride-price would be lowered, and it would be even more difficult for Laban to attract a marriage partner for her. Technically Jacob might be held responsible for rape due to its ambiguous definition and be required to marry Leah. Perhaps for this reason Laban was ruthless in withholding Rachel from Jacob until he agreed to pay the full bride-price of seven years' labor for Leah as well.

This story provides an instructive insight into the ancient Israelite view of human nature: the law covered varieties of illicit sexual encounters but did not apparently envision the possibility that a virgin might deliberately seduce a man. This would jeopardize her bride-price and her reputation. (Yet there are other examples of this in the Old Testament which will be considered in subsequent chapters.)

Not surprisingly Leah's usurpation of Rachel's marriage bed led to substantial problems in the marriage that followed. Leah's frustration at not being considered the chief wife is reflected in the names she chose for her sons. Reuben ("Look, a son") was her firstborn, followed by Simeon ("hearing—the Lord heard I was hated"), Levi ("joined or pledged—perhaps my husband will join with me"), and Judah ("praise the Lord"). Then Leah had no more children for a time (Gen. 29:35).

After Rachel's slave, Bilhah, bore her mistress two sons, Leah's slave Zilpah also bore two sons. Leah named the first Gad ("fortune or troop"), and the second Asher ("happy, blessed") (see Gen. 30:9-13).

At some point, Leah's oldest son, Reuben, returned from the fields with an armful of mandrakes—an oriental fruit believed to aid in conception—and Rachel, ever anxious for a son of her own, asked for some.[29] Leah sneered, "Is it a small matter that thou hast taken my husband? and wouldest thou take away my son's mandrakes also?" (Gen. 30:14). Apparently Jacob had been sleeping excusively with Rachel. But the women struck a bargain. Rachel would receive the coveted fruit and Leah would "hire" the services of Jacob in exchange for the mandrakes.[30]

That evening Leah intercepted Jacob on his way home from the fields. "Thou must come in unto me; for surely I have hired thee with my son's mandrakes," she said. "And he lay with her that night" (Gen. 30:16-18). Leah conceived a son whom she called Issachar ("reward or hire"). Subsequently she bore a sixth son, Zebulun ("honor me or exalt me—now will my husband dwell with me"), and later a daughter named Dinah.

Although Leah ultimately became Jacob's primary wife at the death of her sister, Leah still took pride that Reuben was then acknowledged as Jacob's firstborn. His position added considerable stature to his mother until he lost his rights by sleeping with Rachel's slave Bilhah. Leah recovered her stature at least in part through Judah, her fourth son. In order to understand how and to what extent, it is necessary to understand the nature of the rights of the firstborn.

A certain mystique surrounded firstborn sons in the Old Testament. Clearly the firstborn son had an important position. But the picture is confusing: just who was legally considered firstborn, and what was the nature of his status and prerogatives? It was a question of critical importance to mothers such as Leah, for it not only affected their social status but their economic well-being as well.

Legally the rights of the firstborn included both the birthright and the blessing. In general terms the birthright encompassed certain inheritance rights to physical property. The patriarchal or patrilineal blessing conferred leadership of the family.

The firstborn birthright provided the heir with a double portion of his father's estate, at least from about the seventeenth century B.C. onward.[31] Where the rule of the double portion was followed, a father with five sons would divide his estate into six shares. The firstborn would receive two shares or a full one-third of the estate, while the other brothers would receive only one share or one-sixth of the estate. (Nuzi custom, dating from about 1300 B.C., allowed the firstborn first choice of at least one of his shares.)

The double portion created a support base for the women of the family, who would then look to the birthright son for food, clothing, and shelter. These women included the son's mother, any childless wives of his father, his unmarried sisters, and any sisters returning home because they were divorced or widowed without children. The birthright son had to help his sisters find husbands and provide them with a dowry.

If a family member lost land through debt or foreclosure on a mortgage, the birthright son had the first right to redeem it and restore the family member to his lands.[32] This right of redemption extended also to any family member who may have been sold into slavery for debt. During his father's lifetime, the birthright son also was responsible (under the direction of his father) for the flocks and anything else put under his charge.

The firstborn blessing conveyed headship of the family or patrilineal descent. According to the custom of the time, a man's name became immortal through his sons.[33]

Chief of the sons in a family was the firstborn, and the family genealogy descended from him. From the time of Aaron to the destruction of the Second Temple in 70 A.D., for example, a firstborn blessing among the tribe of Levi included the right to officiate in the temple (Ex. 28:43). While his father lived, the firstborn was responsible for the welfare of his siblings, preparing him for the time when he would be the family leader. If one of his brothers should die leaving a childless widow, he had the first duty of levirate marriage—or to father children with his sister-in-law, whether his father was alive or not. One of his more obscure duties was to avenge the blood of a murdered family member.[34] The firstborn birthright (land) and the firstborn blessing (leadership) were usually bestowed on the same firstborn son—but not always.

The House of Israel claimed descent from such notables as Abraham, Noah, Methuselah, and Enoch back to Adam, but it actually began with Jacob or Israel. Three of his sons—

Reuben, Judah, and Joseph—contended for firstborn rights. The disposition of those rights among the sons of Israel puzzles most modern readers, and the solution to the puzzle is surprising.

Israel had four wives and twelve sons as follows:

The Chief Wife	A Chief Wife	Concubine	Concubine
Rachel	Leah	Bilhah	Zilpah
	1. Reuben		
	2. Simeon		
	3. Levi		
	4. Judah		
		5. Dan	
		6. Naphtali	
			7. Gad
			8. Asher
	9. Issachar		
	10. Zebulun		
11. Joseph			
12. Benjamin			

In legally designating his firstborn, the patriarch was governed by three conventions: the firstborn was (1) the chronological firstborn of the father, (2) the chronological firstborn of the chief wife, or (3) the father's favorite son. In some cultures a chief wife could apparently contract with her husband before marriage that her son would be firstborn regardless of chronology.[35]

The chronological firstborn of Israel was unquestionably Leah's son Reuben, positively identified as such shortly after Rachel's death. The chronicler of Genesis arranged the twelve sons of Jacob in a list with Leah and her six sons first, Rachel and her two sons second, Bilhah and her two sons third, and Zilpah and her two sons fourth. Here Reuben was called "Jacob's firstborn" (Gen. 35:23-26).

Rachel's firstborn son was Joseph. He was not only the first son of the chief wife, but he was also the favorite son of Jacob. By the time Joseph was seventeen, Israel had clearly favored him above the rest and made him a special princely coat (Gen 37:3). Joseph reported dreams in which he was a leader among his brethren and even his parents bowed down to him. His brothers hated him for his dreams, and his father also rebuked him. But Jacob nevertheless "observed the saying" (v. 11), meaning he noted it and remembered its possible significance. His brothers' envy and hatred grew.

Thus Reuben was Israel's chronological firstborn; Joseph was the firstborn of Rachel (Dan, son of Rachel's slave Bilhah, could have been designated Rachel's firstborn if she had so chosen); and Joseph was Israel's favorite son. When Reuben disgraced his position as firstborn, Joseph was the most likely candidate to replace him. When Reuben slept with Bilhah, his father said: "Unstable as water, thou shalt not excel; because thou wentest up to thy father's bed; then defiledst thou it: he went up to my couch" (Gen. 49:4). But Reuben was also disqualified by his general lack of family leadership. He failed to protect his younger brother Joseph at Dothan. Even worse he then attempted to absolve himself of responsibility with lies and subterfuge, presenting Joseph's torn and bloodied coat to Israel as evidence that Joseph was killed by a wild beast through an act of God (37:31).

Jacob thus felt he had cause for depriving Reuben of his birthright. Strikingly he divided Reuben's birthright between two sons. The firstborn birthright was given to Joseph through his sons Ephraim and Manasseh. The firstborn blessing was given to Judah.

Joseph received the birthright because he was the firstborn son of the chief wife Rachel, the favorite son of Jacob, and the worthiest of all the sons. His double portion came to his two sons, each of whom received a land inheritance in Israel. When

Joseph realized that Jacob was dying, he took his sons, Manasseh and Ephraim, to see their grandfather. Israel told Joseph of his visit with God at Luz (Bethel) on his way to Padanaram. God promised Jacob that he would become a multitude of people and that Canaan would be his everlasting possession (Gen. 48:4; 28:19). Jacob then affirmed Ephraim and Manasseh as his sons: "And now thy two sons . . . are mine; as Reuben and Simeon, they shall be mine" (48:5). Later during the blessing Jacob reiterated this new relationship: "God, before whom my fathers Abraham and Isaac did walk, the God which fed me all my life long unto this day, the Angel which redeemed me from all evil, bless the lads; *and let my name be named on them, and the name of my father Abraham and Isaac*; and let them grow into a multitude in the midst of the earth" (vv. 15-16, italics added).

Joseph presented both Manasseh and Ephraim at Israel's bedside for a blessing. He arranged the boys so that Israel could easily place his right hand on Manasseh's head as befitted the firstborn and his left hand on Ephraim's head. However, Israel crossed his hands, placing his right hand on Ephraim's head and his left hand on Manasseh's and proceeded to bless them. Joseph objected, reminding Israel that Manesseh was the firstborn. But Jacob refused the readjustment, "I know it, my son, I know it: he [Manesseh] shall also become a people and he also shall be great: but truly his younger brother shall be greater than he, and his seed shall become a multitude of nations" (Gen. 48:19). Jacob further confirmed, "I have given to thee one portion above thy brethren" (v. 22). Thus Joseph was given the double portion, and his firstborn birthright was given to Ephraim, his second son and now Jacob's adopted son. This ordination of a second-born adopted son as firstborn in the presence of other biological sons follows no known convention, which is probably why it was deemed significant enough to recount in detail in the Bible. We may deduce from this story that a patriarch could nominate anyone he liked as his firstborn.

Rachel's other legal sons through Bilhah—Dan and Naphtali—and Leah's sons through Zilpah—Gad and Asher—are the only secondary sons recorded in the book of Genesis who were raised to the status of primary sons or full heirs. The legal convention for this enfranchisement is not known, but control of the procedure must have been tied to ownership. Wives controlled their slaves and the children of their slaves, and men did the same.[36]

In the case of Dan and Naphtali, after Rachel's death, Jacob enfranchised them at his discretion. Leah would have had no reason to refuse, raising the number of "her" sons to eight.

It does not seem to have been necessary for Leah or Rachel to adopt these four sons by contract. Although we do not know what legal formality was required, it may have been as simple as pronouncing each one "my son" before witnesses and enfranchising them with all the rights and obligations of heirs.

Dan, Naphtali, Gad, and Asher received land inheritances equal to those of Jacob's other sons, but his blessings to them were among the shortest he gave to any of his sons (Gen. 49:17-21).

When Jacob blessed Judah, his fourth son by Leah, he gave him the firstborn patriarchal or patrilineal blessing. He blessed Judah that he would be a leader and a lawgiver: "The sceptre shall not depart from Judah, nor a lawgiver from between his feet, until Shiloh come" (Gen. 49:10).

The author of 1 Chronicles confirms: "Now the sons of Reuben the firstborn of Israel, (for he was the firstborn; but, forasmuch as he defiled his father's bed, his *birthright* was given unto the sons of Joseph the son of Israel: and *the genealogy is not to be reckoned after the birthright*. For Judah prevailed above his brethren, and of him came the *chief ruler*; but the *birthright was Joseph's*). . . ." (5:1-2 emphasis added). Though the birthright or double-portion inheritance was given to the sons of Joseph, the genealogy was not to be reckoned after them but after Judah, who would have the rights of leadership over Israel until the coming of Messiah.

Thus in a very real sense, Leah became a co-chief wife with Rachel through their sons who shared the firstborn rights.

Bilhah

Bilhah was a victim. We first read of her at Rachel's wedding where we learn she was a chattel—Rachel's dowry, a gift from Laban. Thus she was Rachel's handmaid—her personal servant or slave. Years later she was sent to Jacob's bed (as a legal slave-wife) to bear children for Rachel. After Rachel's death she is no longer called an "amah" (handmaid) but a "pilegesh" (concubine), meaning she was no longer a slave-wife but a free woman (Gen. 35:22). In her new-found freedom, she was seduced by Reuben who lost his firstborn rights by his conduct.

Borrowed from foreign sources, concubinage was practiced only by Hebrews wealthy enough to own slaves.[37] As slavery died out by the time of the Babylonian captivity, so did concubinage. Not that all concubines were slaves. Any woman who was married without exchange of property or contract, or without certain clauses in her marriage contract, was a concubine.[38]

Most concubines in Israel of whom we have record were non-Hebrews who became concubines (pilegeshim) by being freed from slavery upon the death of their mistress or husband. If the slave was not freed, she was known as a handmaid (amah) or a slave-wife. Slave-wives when freed were concubines and their children were also freed.[39] If the chief wife had no children except those born to the concubine, then those children would be heirs to the estate. If the chief wife had children, then the concubine's sons would not inherit unless the father recognized them during his lifetime.[40] The status of a concubine's daughter is not known. No statute deals with it, but she would presumably be dowered as a daughter and suitably married. Depending on what she brought into the marriage as part of the contract and/or consideration, a concubine could be high-caste or low-caste.[41]

We know nothing of Bilhah's background. The origin of her name is unknown,[42] though William Smith suggests it means "timid, bashful."[43] Since her name has foreign origins, she was probably a permanent slave, likely captured in a war or raid. Another reasonable assumption is that she was younger than her mistress.

The story's sketchiness conceals its pathos. As a slave Rachel permitted Bilhah sexual access to Jacob until she had borne two sons, Dan and Naphtali,[44] then this apparently fertile woman had no more children, no doubt because Rachel denied her further sexual relations. (Similarly, Zilpah bore two children within a short time of her marriage to Jacob.)

Several centuries later a Mosaic statute would require a husband to continue his marital duty to his concubine (Ex. 21:10). However, no earlier statute affirms such a custom, and no ancient statute preserves any marital rights for slave-wives.

When Jacob blessed his sons he chastened Reuben for defiling his (Jacob's) marital bed. According to the pseudepigraphical Testament of the Twelve Patriarchs, Reuben claimed to have witnessed Bilhah bathing naked and became consumed by desire. He followed her as she retired to her bed. She was drunk, and he took her without her assent.[45]

Whether she was conscious, consenting, or unaware, Reuben had committed a crime as well as a moral violation. If Bilhah had still been a slave, it would not have been a capital offense because a slave was property not legally a person. Since Bilhah had borne Jacob two sons, and was a concubine, the offense was adultery. Even consensual relations with a concubine was a capital crime.

It is not difficult to imagine Bilhah as a woman who may have longed for an independent relationship with Jacob as a wife and may have wished for more children. It is possible that she was a willing partner to Reuben, although the fact that she does not seem to have been punished lends credence to the pseudepigraphical tale, making her an unequivocal victim.

According to ancient Near Eastern law, whatever punishment Jacob decreed for his wife Bilhah would also extend to Reuben. Penalties for adultery involving free married women included death, slavery, mutilation (cutting off the nose and/or ears), shaving the head and pubic area, the humiliation of being led naked through town (signifying disinheritance), or any combination of the above.[46] A man who committed adultery risked castration under some codes.[47] Of course, forgiveness of the guilty parties was also an option.

As far as we know, Jacob chose not to punish his errant concubine, Bilhah, in any way and only punished Reuben, his eldest son, by denying him the firstborn birthright and blessing.

Notes

1. Josephus, "Antiquities of the Jews," in *Josephus: Complete Works*, trans. William Whiston (1960; rprt., Grand Rapids, MI: Kregel Publications, 1972), 41.

2. Another example would be Moses meeting the daughters of Jethro at the well—one of whom he married.

3. The following conversation is a paraphrase of their interchange taken from the account in Josephus, "Antiquities of the Jews," 41.

4. Cross-cousins are the son and daughter of a sister and brother.

5. Gen. 29:14. According to David Daube, this language and the invitation to dwell in Laban's home indicate a close family

relationship; see "Jacob's Reception by Laban," *Journal of Semitic Studies* 1 (Jan. 1956): 60. R. David Freedman agrees: "The idiomatic meaning in the Bible of 'bone and flesh' is 'very close relative,' 'one of us'—in effect, 'our equal.' For example, when Laban refers to Jacob as 'my bone and my flesh' in Genesis 29:14, he provides Jacob with free hospitality. But in verse 15, where Jacob is demoted to *ah* (brother, kinsman), he has to work for his keep" ("Woman, A Power Equal to Man," *Biblical Archaeology Review* 9 [Jan.-Feb. 1983], 1:58).

6. See Louis M. Epstein, *The Jewish Marriage Contract* (New York: Arno Press, 1973), 59.

7. See G. R. Driver and J. C. Miles, eds., *The Babylonian Laws*, 2 vols. (Oxford: Oxford University Press, 1968,) 1:259-65; 2:51.

8. Epstein, *Jewish Marriage Contract*, 60.

9. Paul A. Kruger, "The Hem of the Garment in Marriage," *Journal of Northwest Semitic Languages* 12 (1984): 79-86.

10. Ze'ev Falk, *Jewish Matrimonial Law in the Middle Ages* (London: Oxford University Press, 1966), 150; Driver and Miles, *The Babylonian Laws*, 1:265n1.

11. One of the many interesting questions raised by this narrative is how much did Jacob actually pay?

A minimum annual wage for an assistant shepherd was about ten shekels of silver in both Eshnunna and Babylonian law; see Barry L. Eichler, *Indenture at Nuzi: The Personal Tidennutu Contract and its Mesopotamian Analogues* (London: Yale University Press, 1973), 86; Laws of Eshnunna 11, in Reuven Yaron, *The Laws of Eshnunna* (Jerusalem: Magnes Press, 1969), 25; Driver and Miles, *The Babylonian Laws*, 471. As a master shepherd, Jacob would customarily be entitled to 15-20 percent of the increase of the flock for wages as well as food and clothing from the owner. Although the master shepherd absorbed the losses from natural death, disease, predators, and marauders, the possibilities of reward for a master shepherd were much greater than ten shekels of silver per year.

The biblical bride-price of fifty shekels of silver (Deut. 22:29) may include a penalty because of the prospective husband's wrongdoing in this case. Three old Babylonian marriage contracts involv-

59

ing high-class temple priestesses recorded bride-prices of one-half *maneh*, or thirty shekels of silver, in one contract and one-third *maneh*, or twenty shekels, in two other contracts; see Driver and Miles, *The Babylonian Laws*, 1:253-59.

The prophet Hosea paid a bride-price of fifteen shekels of silver and one and one-half homers of barley—a total of just over seventeen shekels of silver—but this price may have been exceptionally low because his wife is designated as a "harlot" and was at least a divorcee (Hos. 3:1-3). A seventh-century B.C. marriage contract provided for a bride-price of sixteen shekels of silver; see John Van Seters, *Abraham in History and Tradition* (New Haven, CT: Yale University Press, 1975), 83. Fifth-century B.C. contracts from Elephantine specify five and ten shekels of silver; see Reuven Yaron, *Introduction to the Law of the Aramaic Papyri* (Oxford: Clarendon Press, 1961), 47.

Although bride-prices varied in different times and locales, Jacob's bride-price was nothing to be ashamed of. At the absolute minimum he paid seventy shekels of silver as a bride-price (seven years times ten shekels). This was sufficient to purchase from two to three slaves and exceeded the usual and customary bride-price.

12. It was a custom at the time and for many centuries thereafter (for example, Samson's marriage in Judges 14:17) to observe a seven-day marriage feast so that nomadic family and friends could come together and get reacquainted before leaving again for remote areas.

13. Menachem Elon, *The Principles of Jewish Law* (Jerusalem: Keter Publishing House Jerusalem Ltd., 1975), 390; Epstein, *Jewish Marriage Contract*, 90-91.

14. Ibid., 94.

15. The Code of Hammurabi, for example, required the husband to pay an additional amount similar to the bride-price; see Code of Hammurabi 138, in Driver and Miles, *The Babylonian Laws*, 2:55.

16. Epstein, *Jewish Marriage Contract*, 100.

17. Katarzyna Grosz, "Dowry and Brideprice in Nuzi," in *Studies on the Civilization and Culture of Nuzi and the Hurrians in Honor of Ernest R. Bacheman*, ed. M. A. Morrison and D. I. Owen (Winona

Lake, IN: Eisenbraun, 1981), 161-77.

18. Epstein, *Marriage Laws in the Bible and Talmud*, 5.

19. Ibid. Gideon, a judge in Israel, had seventy-one sons, "for he had many wives" (Judges 8:30-31). A census of Nuzi households (mid-second millennium B.C.) revealed that about 25 percent had two or more wives. This is a little surprising in light of earlier Babylonian statutory law that clearly prohibited polygyny except when a wife was barren or ill and therefore incapable of either bearing children or having sexual relations; see L. M. Muntingh, "The Social and Legal Status of a Free Ugaritic Female," *Journal of Near Eastern Studies* 26 (1967): 102; Code of Hammurabi 144 and 148, in Driver and Miles, *The Babylonian Laws*. 2:57-59.

However, numerous old Babylonian marriage contracts exist in which a man married two women at the same time. In each case the wives were called "sisters" (though it is not clear that they were biological sisters) and one was a primary wife while the second had a lower status—either as a concubine or slave-wife with the responsibility of serving the first. Here is an example of such a contract from about 1800 B.C.:

> Iltani is the sister of Taram-Sagila. Warad-Shamash son of Ili-ennam has taken them from their father Shamash-TA-tum for marriage. As for Iltani, her sister, "Whenever she is angry she shall be angry, whenever she is friendly, she shall be friendly." She shall carry her chair to the temple of Marduk. As many children as she has borne and will bear are their children, but (if) she (T.) says to her sister Iltani, "You are not my sister," [she will take the hand of her] son [and leave]. [(And) if Iltani s]ay[s to her sister Taram-Sagila] "Y[ou are not my sister"] she will shave her and sell her. And (if) Warad-Shamash says to his wives, "You are not my wives," he shall pay 1 mina of silver. And (if) they say to their husband Warad-Shamash, "You are not our husband," they will bind them and cast them into the river (Raymond Westbrook, "Old Babylonian Marriage Law," vol. 1, Ph.d.

diss., University of Michigan at Ann Arbor, 1982, 205, also 247, 252).

20. Louis M. Epstein, *Marriage Laws in the Bible and Talmud* (1942; rprt. New York: Johnson Reprint Corporation, 1968), 37.

21. "When a seignior married a woman and a fever has then seized her, if he has made up his mind to marry another, he may marry (her), without divorcing his wife whom the fever seized; she shall live in the house which he built and he shall continue to support her as long as she lives." Code of Hammurabi 148, in James B. Pritchard, ed., *Ancient Near Eastern Texts* (Princeton, NJ: Princeton University Press, 1969), 172; see also Code of Hammurabi 145; Muntingh, "Free Ugaritic Female," 102.

22. Code of Hammurabi 170-71, in Driver and Miles, *The Bablyonian Laws*, 2: 65-67.

23. See, for example, Middle Assyrian Law A 46 in Pritchard, *Ancient Near Eastern Texts*, 184.

24. William Gesenius, *A Hebrew and English Lexicon of the Old Testament*, eds. F. Brown, S. R. Driver, and C. A. Briggs (Oxford: Clarendon Press, 1976), 275.

25. "If a free man cohabits with (several) slave-girls, sisters and their mother, there shall be no punishment. If blood-relations sleep with (the same) free woman, there shall be no punishment. If father and son sleep with (the same) slave-girl or harlot, there shall be no punishment." Hittite Law 194, in Pritchard, *Ancient Near Eastern Texts*, 196.

26. ". . . if a seignior took the virgin by force and ravished her, either in the midst of the city or in the open country or at night in the street or in a granary or at the city festival, the father of the virgin shall take the wife of the virgin's ravisher and give her to be ravished; he shall not return her to her husband (but) take her"; Middle Assyrian Law A 55, in ibid., 185.

27. "If the virgin has given herself to the seignior, the seignior shall (so) swear and they shall not touch his wife; the seducer shall give the (extra) third in silver as the value of a virgin (and) the father shall treat his daughter as he wishes." Middle Assyrian Law A 56, ibid., 185.

28. Epstein, *Jewish Marriage Contract*, 60.

29. C. F. Keil and F. Delitzsch, *Commentary on the Old Testament*, 10 vol. (Grand Rapids, MI: William B. Eerdmans Publishing Company, 1985), 1:289.

30. See David Daube, *Studies in Biblical Law* (New York: KTAV Publishing House, 1969), 19-24, for an excellent insight into this scenario.

31. I have found no evidence anywhere that a firstborn son ever inherited the entire estate where he had brothers of equal status. Generally sons of equal status inherited equally, and the double portion was an exception.

32. H. H. Rowley, "The Marriage of Ruth," *Harvard Theological Review* 40 (1947): 85.

33. Driver and Miles, *The Babylonian Laws*, 1:330.

34. Rowley, "The Marriage of Ruth," 85.

35. For example, an Old Babylonian contract stipulates: "If . . . (another wife) to Irihalpa gives birth to a son first and after that Naidu {this is her marriage contract} gives birth to a son, the son of Naidu alone shall be the firstborn"; Thomas L. Thompson, *The Historicity of the Patriarchal Narratives* (New York: Walter de Gruyter, 1974), 265.

36. For example, the Code of Hammurabi (secs. 170-71 in Driver and Miles, *The Babylonian Laws*, 2:65) declares that a man may enfranchise sons born to him of *his* slave-female. The Middle Assyrian laws provide for a man to elevate *his* secondary wife to the status of primary wife by veiling her in the presence of five or six witnesses (Middle Assyrian Law A 41, in G. R. Driver and J. C. Miles, eds., *The Assyrian Laws* [Oxford: Clarendon Press, 1935], 409). The Code of Hammurabi, as already discussed, prescribed the punishments a chief wife could inflict on a slave-wife *she* owned who attempted to elevate herself to the status of the chief wife (Code of Hammurabi 146-47, in Driver and Miles, *The Babylonian Laws*, 2:57).

The story of Sarah's dealings with Hagar and Ishmael illustrates that slave-wives and their children remained under the control of the chief wife. She had the power to claim the children as her legal sons, thus making them legal sons or enfranchised heirs of their father.

37. Epstein, *Marriage Laws in the Bible and Talmud*, 34, 37, 39.

38. Ibid., 41, 44; Epstein, *Jewish Marriage Contract*, 9n29.

39. Concubines such as Keturah, who Abraham married after the death of Sarah (Gen. 25:6), were likely free to begin with and were married as concubines so that they would have no claim on the inheritance of Isaac.

40. Driver and Miles, *The Babylonian Laws*, 1:65.

41. Epstein, *Marriage Laws in the Bible and Talmud*, 35.

42. Gesenius, *A Hebrew and English Lexicon*, 117.

43. William Smith, *A Dictionary of the Bible* (Grand Rapids, MI: Zondervan Publishing House, 1972), 93.

44. When Rachel died Bilhah was freed and her slave-wife status was elevated to concubine. But when her sons became full heirs, her status would have changed from low-caste concubine (one without any assets) to a high-caste concubine (one whose sons would have assets with which to support their mother as the need arose).

45. James H. Charlesworth, ed., *The Old Testament Pseudepigrapha*, 2 vols. (Garden City, NY: Doubleday, 1980), 1:783.

46. "If the wife of a seignior has been caught while lying with another man, they shall bind them and throw them into the water. If the husband of the woman wishes to spare his wife, then the king in turn may spare his subject." Code of Hammurabi 129, in Pritchard, *Ancient Near Eastern Texts*, 171.

"Apart from the penalties for [a seignior's wife] which [are prescribed] on the tablet, [when she deserves it], a seignior may pull out (the hair of) his wife, mutilate (or) twist her ears, with no liability attaching to him." Middle Assyrian Law A 59, in ibid., 185.

See also, Hittite Law 198, in ibid., 196; Middle Assyrian Law A 57, in ibid., 185; Kruger, "The Hem of the Garment," 82; Anthony Phillips, "Another Look at Adultery," *Journal of Studies in the Old Testament* 20 (July 1981): 4.

47. "If a seignior has caught a[nother] seignior with his wife, when they have prosecuted him [and] convicted him, they shall put both of them to death, with no liability attaching to him. If, upon catching [him], he has brought him either into the presence of the

king or into the presence of the judges, when they have prosecuted him [and] convicted him, if the woman's husband puts his wife to death, he shall also put the seignior to death, but if he cuts off his wife's nose, he shall turn the seignior into a eunuch and they shall mutilate his whole face. However, if he let his wife go free, they shall let the seignior go free." Middle Assyrian Law A 15, in Pritchard, *Ancient Near Eastern Texts,* 181.

See also Samuel Greengus, "A Textbook Case of Adultery in Ancient Mesopotamia," *Hebrew Union College Annual* 40 (1969): 33.

IV.

METRONYMIC MARRIAGE

I n a metronymic marriage the husband joined his wife's
family, and the children took the name of the mother or her
father. Other indications a marriage was metronymic were the
absence of bride-price, dowry, or contract; the wife remaining
in her father's house; a stipulation that the father's inheritance
passed to the daughter's children'; the use of kinship terms
between father-in-law and son-in-law such as "father" and
"son'"; the husband seeking permission of the father-in-law for
decisions; and similar acts of deference to the father-in-law. In
an *erebu* marriage the groom was adopted into the wife's family
and became a permanent member of her father's household
with the children belonging to the wife's father.' In either case
the husband became subservient to the wife's father.

Rachel and Jacob

Did Rachel and Jacob have such a marriage? The circumstances of Jacob's flight from Padanaram after many years of
service to Rachel's father Laban raise the question.

It seems clear that when Laban hired Jacob as a shepherd
under a contractual arrangement, he did so at least with the

proviso that Jacob would be working for the hand of Rachel not for wages. This arrangement at best deviated from the norm. It seems possible that Laban had no sons at this time, although he did later at the time Jacob wanted to leave Padanaram. If he were without sons he would have had a greater interest in keeping his daughters close to home (Gen. 31:1).

Cyrus Gordon suggests that Laban adopted Jacob by betrothing and marrying him to Rachel. Gordon cites a documented case in a Nuzi community probably two or three centuries after Jacob. The father wanted to provide for his daughter's security by ensuring her access to his estate after his own death, so he adopted a man as his son and then married him to his daughter: "The adoption tablet of Nashwi son of Arshenni. He adopted Wullu son of Puhishenni. As long as Nashwi lived, Wullu shall give (him) food and clothing. When Nashwi dies, Wullu shall be the heir. Should Nashwi beget a son, (the latter) shall divide equally with Wullu but (only) Nashwi's son shall take Nashwi's gods. But if there be no son of Nashwi's, then Wullu shall take Nashwi's gods. And (Nashwi) has given his daughter Nuhuya as wife to Wullu. And if Wullu takes another wife, he forfeits Nashwi's land and buildings. Whoever breaks the contract shall pay one mina of silver (and) one mina of gold."[4]

While this contract provides for the adoption of a son-in-law and the creation of an *erebu* marriage, it does not fit the facts of Jacob's case. Similarly the fact that there was a contract, that Jacob served Laban for fourteen years as a bride-price for both Rachel and Leah, and that each received a handmaid as dowry seems to argue against metronymic marriage. At the end of his bride-price service, Jacob said to Laban, "Give me my wives and my children, for whom I have served thee, and let me go: for thou knowest my service which I have done thee" (Gen. 30:26). Why did Jacob have to request what was already his?

68

Perhaps Jacob was putting Laban on notice. Perhaps Jacob was trying to flatter Laban, knowing that he could not leave without his consent—for practical rather than legal reasons. Laban would later try to justify himself by arguing that Jacob's marriage was a metronymic arrangement. However, I am convinced both men knew that it was not technically so.

Laban responded by persuading Jacob to continue working for him, "for I have learned by experience that the Lord hath blessed me for thy sake" (Gen. 30:27). They negotiated a new contract, and Jacob worked at least six more years (vv. 28-34).

During this additional period, Jacob prospered and "increased exceedingly, and had much cattle, and maidservants, and menservants, and camels, and asses.... And Jacob beheld the countenance of Laban, and behold, it was not toward him as before" (Gen. 30:43; 31:2). The Lord appeared to Jacob and instructed him to return to the land of his fathers (31:3).

Jacob explained this decision to Rachel and Leah: he had served their father faithfully, but Laban had changed his wages ten times. God had intervened, rewarding Jacob with abundance and leaving Laban with little. Rachel and Leah also complained that their father had cheated them—probably out of a proper dowry and bride-price. They agreed that God had consequently taken their father's flocks and given the increase to them and to their children (Gen. 31:16). Their wholehearted support of Jacob indicated that they did not have the feeling that he had become a member of their father's household nor that his children by them were legally Laban's—both characteristics of a metronymic marriage.

Knowing that Laban would never agree to let him leave, Jacob escaped when Laban was off shearing his sheep, taking all of his possessions (Gen. 31:20). Rachel stole the *teraphim* or household gods of her father, a foolish act which enraged Laban and gave him additional cause to pursue Jacob. The Nuzi contract quoted above appears to suggest that the gods were somehow attached to the inheritance rights of sons. However, since they were leaving, it may be that Rachel feared the *teraphim* might help Laban to divine where they had fled.

After three days Laban heard of the departure of Jacob and his daughters. He assembled "his brethren" (Gen. 31:23)—probably his servants and local townsmen—and took up the pursuit. This band seems to have been a sizeable number, for Laban does not bother with tact. Instead he immediately set up a court. Laban was the accuser or plaintiff. Jacob was the accused or defendant. The people, of whom Laban had the greater number, would sit in judgment. Laban wanted to prove that he was justified in pursuing Jacob and forcing him to return to Padanaram.

His complaint included two charges. The first, stated four ways, was the offense of leaving without permission, a violation of the metronymic commitment that required Jacob to recognize Laban as his father and required Jacob's subservience. "Thou hast stolen away unawares to me," Laban said, stressing that he had a right to participate in their departure. "Thou hast . . . carried away my daughters, as captives taken with the sword" (Gen. 31:26), an accusation of kidnapping. "Wherefore didst thou flee away secretly, and steal away from me[?]" (v. 27). Laban was clearly suggesting that Jacob's clandestine behavior proved his guilt. "Thou . . . didst not tell me, that I might have sent thee away with mirth, and with songs, with tabret, and with harp. And hast not suffered me to kiss my sons and my daughters" (vv. 27-28). Laban speaks in possessives here, accentuating his claim to this family, as though Jacob's children were his own flesh and blood as much as Rachel and Leah were. Second, he presented his most valid legal complaint, "Wherefore hast thou stolen my gods?" (v. 30)

Jacob was stunned. He knew nothing of any stolen gods, nor did he believe anyone in his entourage had them. Therefore, in the presence of all, he articulated the law regarding the theft of sacred things: "With whomsoever thou findest thy gods, let him not live."[5] Thus Jacob himself passed the death sentence on Rachel.

Laban searched the camp with vigor, beginning at Jacob's tent. Then he went into the slave-wives tents. Next he searched Leah's tent and finally Rachel's. By now he must have been very anxious because theft of the gods was his most valid charge. If he could find them, he would not need to prove the metronymic marriage charge and could compel Jacob to return to Padamaram with his family and flocks.

As he entered Rachel's tent Rachel feigned her menstrual period and sat on the container where she had hidden the gods, thereby contaminating the area and preventing a search. Laban searched the rest of the tent diligently but found nothing.

When the court reconvened, Jacob vented years of pent-up righteous indignation as he refuted Laban's charges. He first challenged Laban to put all he had found that was his before the witnesses/court (Gen. 31:37). When Laban was unable to produce the *teraphim*, the capital offense charge was dropped. Then Jacob focused on his contract, how he had served Laban and fulfilled his contract more faithfully than was required. If he could convince the witnesses that his was a contract relationship, the charge of metronymic marriage would not stand up.

"And Jacob was wroth, and chode with Laban" (Gen. 31:36). Before his shepherd peers Jacob forcefully outlined his compliance with the contract and Laban's failure to comply. During the twenty years of contracts, Jacob was attentive during the birthing season so that no newborn lambs or kids were lost. He did not eat the young rams. He deducted from his increase animals lost through an act of God (which he did not have to replace), animals stolen by day (which he was obligated to replace), or animals stolen by night (which he was not

71

obligated to replace). He suffered heat and cold to preserve the flocks, suggesting that Laban had not supplied proper clothing as was his due. And Laban for his part had used his power unjustly in changing his wages ten times and plotting, except for the intervention of God, to strip Jacob of all that he had lawfully earned and send him away empty (vv. 38-42).

Laban in a last effort to save face reiterated his argument for a metronymic interpretation of Jacob's marriages, which would mean that Jacob's property was rightfully his own: "These daughters are my daughters, and these children are my children, and these cattle are my cattle, and all that thou seest is mine" (Gen. 31:43). However, he must have known that the convened court would not uphold him. Nothing but the use of force would maintain his claim. Therefore, Laban conceded defeat and invited Jacob to enter into a final covenant with him. They agreed never to harm each other (Gen. 31:52). Laban added language that was standard in ancient marriage contracts, typically written by the father of the bride: if Jacob abused his wives or took additional wives, Laban would not be bound by the covenant (v. 50).

The next day Laban arose, kissed his daughters and grandchildren, and returned home. Thus the question of the metronymic marriages of Jacob was put to rest.

Rahab: Harlot of Jericho

Rahab was called a "harlot" (Jos. 2:1), yet she was later honored by New Testament writers Paul (Heb. 11:31) and James (Jas. 2:25) as a woman of great faith. Furthermore, commentators identify her with Rachab (Matt. 1:5), the mother of Boaz.[6] If this is so, her historical importance extends far beyond the city of Jericho.

Still, we must also point out that there is no evidence that at the time of this narrative Rahab was married. However, she represents an interesting class of women, who on other occasions participated in a form of metronymic marriage. Her story provides a pattern which we can assume applies to women whose stories we do not have.

When Joshua invaded Canaan the first city in his path was Jericho. He sent two spies ahead to reconnoiter the city. They found shelter in Rahab's house. Her house must have been some sort of public establishment, for they ate and lodged with her (Jos. 2:1). She was called a harlot (*zonah* in Hebrew; Jos. 2:1).[7] Her Babylonian counterparts during the time of Hammurabi[8] and a century and a half later under Ammisaduqa[9] were translated as "ale-wives." Such women chose not to belong to traditional family units. These women owned their own public establishments, where they offered lodging, meals, alcoholic beverages, and sometimes themselves. They contracted metronymic marriage-like liaisons with their patrons and sometimes "married" more than one patron—something called "nair polyandry".[10] Such a relationship safeguarded the woman's independence. The visiting patron had the privilege of the woman's bedroom, but all the property, including any that he might bring to the relationship and any children born of their union, belonged to her and could be inherited by her father's descendants.

These women were not generally held in high esteem, for the Old Babylonian law dealt harshly with them. The law regulated the prices they could charge for alcoholic beverages[11] and set the death penalty for dishonesty[12] or overcharging.[13] Priestesses were burned to death if caught plying their trade as sacral prostitutes in a wine shop[14] or even consuming alcohol in a tavern.[15]

The Code of Hammurabi subjected female innkeepers or ale-wives to additional royal regulation. Recognized as sources of information valuable to the king, the women were required to report and even arrest suspicious visitors. Section 109 records, "If outlaws have congregated in the establishment of a woman wine seller and she has not arrested those outlaws and did not take them to the palace, that wine seller shall be put to death."[16]

If such a statute were in force at the time of Rahab and if her profession were that of an ale-wife, it would explain why the king of Jericho sent men to ask her about the Israelite spies. She admitted that they had come to her but lied and said they had left. Actually they were hiding on her roof under sheaves of flax. She breached her legal obligation to the king and supported the spies. Why? It appears that she, a Canaanite, had become converted to the God of Israel. As she told the spies: "I know that the Lord hath given you the land, and that your terror is fallen upon us, and that all the inhabitants of the land faint because of you. For we have heard how the Lord dried up the water of the Red Sea for you, when ye came out of Egypt; and what ye did unto the two kings of the Amorites, that were on the other side Jordan, Sihon and Og, whom ye utterly destroyed. And as soon as we had heard these things, our hearts did melt, neither did there remain any more courage in any man, because of you: *for the Lord your God, he is God in heaven above, and in earth beneath*" (Jos. 2:9-11; italics added).

Rahab placed the two Israelites under oath to spare her and her family because she protected them: "Swear unto me by the Lord, since ye will also shew kindness unto my father's house, and give me a true token: And that ye will save alive my father, and my mother, and my brethren, and my sisters, and all that they have, and deliver our lives from death" (Jos. 2:12-13).

The spies agreed ("our life for yours"; Jos 2:14) and told her to identify her house by a scarlet cloth in her window and to have all her family inside during the attack. Joshua ratified this agreement and charged his army to spare Rahab and her family (6:17). On the day the walls of Jericho fell, all the men,

women, and children of the city were slain except for Rahab
and her family (v. 23).

According to Jewish tradition, Rahab was one of the four
most beautiful women in history along with Sarah, Abigail,
and Esther. This same tradition holds that after the destruction
of Jericho, Rahab married Joshua and became the progenitor
of at least eight prophets including Jeremiah.[17] Christian
tradition, documented in the New Testament (Matt. 1:5),
asserts that she married Salmon and became the mother of
Boaz. Whatever her past may have been, she earned the acclaim
of Christians and Jews alike.

Notes

1. John Van Seters, "Jacob's Marriages," *Harvard Theological
Review* 62 (1969): 386.

2. Ibid., 390.

3. R. T. O'Callahan, "Historical Parallels to Patriarchal Social
Custom," *Catholic Biblical Quarterly* 6 (1944): 399.

4. Cyrus Gordon, "Biblical Cistons and the Nuzu Tablets," *The
Biblical Archeologist* 3 (1940): 1:5.

5. Gen. 31:32; see, for example, Code of Hammurabi 6, in James
B. Pritchard, ed., *Ancient Near Eastern Texts* (Princeton, NJ: Princeton University Press, 1969), 166.

6. Adam Clarke, *The Holy Bible Containing the Old And New
Testaments with a Commentary and Critical Notes* (Nashville, TN:
Abingdon Press, 1830), 2: 41; R. F. Brown, "Rachab in Mt. 1, 5
Probably Is Rahab of Jericho," *Biblica* 63 (1982): 79; contra J. D.
Quinn, "Is PAXAB in Mt. 1, 5 Rahab of Jericho?" *Biblica* 62 (1981):
225.

7. R. L. Harris, G. L. Archer, Jr., and B. K. Waltke, eds.,
Theological Wordbook of the Old Testament (Chicago: Moody Press,
1980), 246.

8. G. R. Driver and J. C. Miles, eds., *The Babylonian Laws*, 2
vols. (Oxford: Oxford University Press, 1968), 1:202-205.

WOMEN'S RIGHTS IN OLD TESTAMENT TIMES

9. Ibid., 2:45.

10. Lewis M. Epstein, *Sex Laws and Customs in Judaism* (New York: KTAV Publishing House, Inc., 1967), 159-61. Nair polyandry is "a metronymic family headed by the wife, who maintains her own apartment in the midst of her own tribe and has a number of husbands visiting her successively for a specific period of time" (ibid., 160).

11. "If an ale-wife has given 60 *sila* of coarse liquor on credit, at the harvest she shall take 50 *sila* of corn." Code of Hammurabi 111, in Driver and Miles, *The Babylonian Laws*, 2:45.

12. "A taverness or merchant who [. . .] dishonest weight shall die." Edict of Ammisaduqa 18, in Pritchard, *Ancient Near Eastern Texts*, 528.

13. "If an ale-wife does not accept grain for the price of liquor (but) accepts silver by the heavy weight or (if) she reduces the value of beer (given) against the value of corn (received), they shall convict that ale-wife and cast her into the water." Code of Hammurabi 108, in Driver and Miles, *The Babylonian Laws*, 2:45.

14. Ibid., 1:206.

15. "If a priestess (or) a high-priestess, who is not dwelling in a cloister, opens an ale-house or enters an ale-house for liquor, they shall burn that woman." Code of Hammurabi 110, in Driver and Miles, *The Babylonian Laws*, 2:45.

16. Code of Hammurabi 109 in Pritchard, *Ancient Near Eastern Texts*, 170.

17. Megillah 14b-15a, in I. Epstein, ed. and trans., *The Babylonian Talmud* (London: Soncino Press, 1948), 86.

V.

Sarai/Sarah's Household

Sarai

Who was Sarai? We know she was the wife of Abraham. But she was also represented to Pharaoh as Abraham's sister. To Abimelech Abraham said, "And yet indeed she is my sister; she is the daughter of my father, but not the daughter of my mother; and she became my wife" (Gen. 20:12). This riddle would suggest that Terah had more than one wife by whom he had children and Abraham married a half-sister—unheard of among the common people of Mesopotamia. The only ones who married their sisters were the Pharaohs of Egypt—and this because gods, which the Pharaohs were esteemed to be, could only marry goddesses.

Perhaps Josephus holds the key to this mystery. According to him, Sarai, or Sarah,[1] was born to Haran, the brother of Abram in a city of the Chaldeans called Ur.[2] This would make her Abram's niece. According to the account in Genesis 11:28-29, Haran died before the marriage of Abram and Sarai. If in this interval Terah adopted Sarai, a common practice at the time, then Sarai would have been Abram's legal sister at the time of her marriage and yet not proscribed from marriage because her blood relationship was niece. Further evidence that this might be the case is the fact that Nahor, Abraham's other brother, married Milcah, another daughter of Haran and according to Josephus a sister to Sarai.

Sarai and Abram moved from Ur to Haran, situated in southern Turkey just north of the Syrian border. Here her husband received his first biblically recorded revelation from God. He was told to leave Haran and go to a land which God would show him. He would become a great nation, and through him all nations of the earth would be blessed (Gen. 12:1-3). The revelation that Abram would become a great nation must have been a great surprise to Sarai, for at sixty-five she had not been able to conceive.

Sarai and Abram left for Canaan accompanied by Lot. If Sarai was the daughter of Haran, then Lot was Sarai's brother. They traveled to the promised land of Canaan only to find it ravaged by drought. Abram built an altar at Shechem, where the Lord again appeared and confirmed that the land was his (Gen. 12:6-7). Later at Bethel Abram again called upon God (v. 8). We do not know what occurred, but subsequently Abram left Canaan and traveled to Egypt, presumably at divine direction.

The Egyptian episode is puzzling. In Egypt Abram presented himself and Sarai as brother and sister rather than as husband and wife (Gen. 12:12-13). There is no evidence that the Egyptians were in the habit of killing husbands to obtain their wives, nor was this happening in any other contemporary civilization. Abram was forewarned that he would run into trouble in Egypt, for he was able to prophetically assure Sarai, "Say, I pray thee, thou art my sister: that it may be well with me for thy sake; and my soul shall live because of thee" (v. 13).

Sarai's beauty impressed "the Egyptians," specifically "the princes also of Pharaoh" who "commended her before Pharaoh." It is not clear whether Pharaoh saw her before making the decision to have her "taken into Pharaoh's house," meaning his harem (Gen. 13:14-15). To Abram he paid a magnificent bride-price of "sheep, and oxen, and he asses, and menservants, and maidservants, and she asses, and camels" (12:16). Presumably here Sarai also received her maidservant Hagar. Then evidently before Sarai could be violated, an outbreak of "great plagues" on "Pharaoh and his house" somehow revealed to Pharaoh that she was Abram's wife (vv. 17-18).

Pharaoh protested with some justification to Abram, "Why didst thou not tell me that she was thy wife?" But he sent Abram away with "all that he had" (Gen. 12:20), allowing him to keep the bride-price as well. This is puzzling, as Abram had received the bride-price under fraudulent pretenses and should have returned it.

There are two possible reasons why. First, Pharaoh's priests may have told him that Abram's God was afflicting him and his people because of his lust for Sarai. Adultery under Egyptian law—even unintended adultery—was "the great sin"[3] and carried the death penalty.[4] Pharaoh may have allowed Abram to retain the bride-price as his penance. Middle Assyrian law provides a precedent for mistaken involvement with a married woman. According to tablet A 22, if a man took a woman with him on a journey and was not aware that she was married, he had to pay a major fine to her husband and possibly forfeit his life if he had had relations with her.[5]

A second reason Abram was allowed to keep his property may have been as compensation for teaching Egyptian scholars and priests arithmetic and astronomy, thus being accepted as a man of great sagacity.[6]

Abram had a trusted servant whose name according to the scriptural account was Eliezer of Damascus, a houseborn slave. At some time prior to Sarai's seventy-fifth year, she acquiesced to the adoption of Eliezer. The scriptural narrative does not mention Eliezer's adoption or a contract, but Abram spoke of him as his "heir" (Gen. 15:3).

It is improbable that Abram would have used this term carelessly, especially in such a setting. Although we do not know what Abram's legal understanding was, it seems unlikely that a slave could have been referred to as an heir unless he had been so designated by contract.[7] If Eliezer had not been adopted, Abram would have referred to his brothers or his nephews such as Lot as his heirs.

It was not uncommon in most ancient Near East jurisdictions for a childless couple to adopt a son.[8] In my view Sarai agreed to the adoption of Eliezer because it was a more acceptable option to her than providing her husband with a second wife.[9] But an adopted son always ran the risk of being replaced by a biological son, although only rarely was an adopted son disinherited completely.[10]

After Abram was told by God that he had erred in assuming he could make Eliezer his heir, he was further informed, "(B)ut he that shall come forth out of thine own bowels shall be thine heir" (Gen. 15:4). Then Sarai, still barren, could see no other way to provide her husband with an heir of his body except to present her slave Hagar to him to be his second wife.[11] Marriage contracts granting a woman the right to provide her husband with a slave to bear children were not without precedent in Old Babylon. The husband still had the final say as to whether he would accept the maid from his wife, but if the contract was clear on the matter, the choice of which maid was not his.[12]

Slavery was widely practiced anciently. Freemen or free-women could own male or female slaves without any known limitations. Existing documents show that women owned male slaves, although biblical legislation and contemporary legal codes deal only with male ownership of slaves of both sexes.[13] Numerous marriage contracts, bills of sale, and court records indicate that it was common for women to own female slaves from the earliest times. If a wife was barren, she could acquire a child by having her husband impregnate her slave. If she did not have a slave, her husband had the right to marry a second wife.[14]

In one Old Babylonian contract, a husband and wife together purchased a slave named Shamash-nuri for five shekels of silver. To the husband she was a wife (slave-wife); to the wife she was a slave. If Shamash-nuri "despised" her mistress, she could be shaved and sold as a slave.[15] Being a slave-wife was a legal status. If she became a concubine, it meant that she had gained her freedom.[16] The slave-wife could be manumitted voluntarily by her owner(s). In the case of divorce or upon her husband's death, she became automatically free.[17] Thus in this one case, a slave's right to freedom overrode the wife's property right. The husband and the chief wife together could offer voluntary manumission at any time.[18]

Sarai took the initiative in the matter of Hagar. Possibly her marriage contract obligated her to do so. Upon the birth of Ishmael, Eliezer dropped from primary heir to secondary heir, because if a chief wife had no son, a son from a concubine or slave-wife was the heir.[19] At Ishmael's birth then, Ishmael became the primary heir apparent. When Isaac was born, Isaac became the primary heir, and Ishmael was relegated to the position of secondary heir, inheriting only if Isaac died before him and had no children.

Unwisely, Hagar as soon as she became pregnant "despised" Sarai (Gen. 15:4). This was apparently a sufficiently common problem that the Code of Hammurabi (and the much earlier Laws of Ur-Nammu) had a provision for it. When a slave-wife upon conceiving or bearing children tried to elevate herself to the status of her mistress, her mistress could brand her with a slave mark and return her to the rank of slave.[20] She would no longer enjoy the special benefits and prestige of being

81

the husband's consort and would be relegated to whatever lowly slave-tasks her mistress prescribed for her. There is no evidence Hagar would lose her right to be free upon the husband's death or in the event she was divorced—or cast out. If the misbehaving slave-wife had not conceived or borne children, her mistress could sell her.[21]

Sarai, angered by Hagar's behavior, suggested to Abram that he might share some blame ("My wrong be upon thee"; Gen. 15:5). Abram simply reminded her of the law: "Behold, thy maid is in thy hand; do to her as it pleaseth thee" (v. 6). Sarai was the chief wife, and the slave was her property.

The record says that Sarai "dealt hardly" with Hagar (Gen. 15:6). We do not know exactly what Sarai did. In addition to the branding and demotion (humiliation) allowed by the Code of Hammurabi, the Ur-Nammu code allowed an owner to scour the mouth of an insolent slave with a quart of salt.[22] Other forms of corporal punishment such as flogging were available. Hagar fled into the wilderness, becoming a runaway slave. It seems unlikely that she could have eluded pursuit from trained hunters, so probably Sarai ordered that she be allowed to go.

The narrative continues: An angel found Hagar in the desert by a well, confirmed that she would bear a son and instructed her to "return to thy mistress, and submit thyself under her hands" (Gen. 16:9). Hagar returned to camp and reconciled herself with Sarai, was reinstated as slave-wife, and bore the eighty-six-year-old Abram a son whom he named Ishmael. Hagar bore no further children, and it is reasonable to assume that Sarai withdrew her slave from any further connubial relations with Abram.

The laws of the time favored the inheritance of biological sons over adoptive sons whether by slave-wives, concubines, or harlots.[23] According to Middle Assyrian law dating from about four hundred years later and from the earlier Code of

Lipit-Ishtar, if such a son was a man's only biological son, he would be his sole heir.[24]

Was Ishmael, son of a slave-wife, Abram's firstborn? Chronologically speaking he was. But according to the Code of Hammurabi dating from about 1750 B.C.,[25] Abram had to acknowledge Ishmael as his heir for him to be considered firstborn. In many verses of Genesis, Ishmael is called the son of Abraham, and at least one historian interprets these passages to mean that Abraham had enfranchised Ishmael with heir status.[26] However, nowhere in the record does Abraham call Ishmael "my son" or "my child" in the legal vernacular necessary to raise Ishmael to the status of heir. Further, Code of Hammurabi section 170 cited above suggests that the father had the right to so designate sons born to him of "his female slave" and makes no mention of any rights the father had regarding his children by his wife's female slave.

The scriptural record though not specific allows us to hypothesize that Abraham wanted to acknowledge Ishmael as his heir but that Sarah prevented him, even though she had initially given Hagar to Abraham for the purpose of conceiving a child. Obviously she had changed her mind at some point. In the only scriptural passage in which Sarah's exact words are quoted about Ishmael, she calls him "the son of this bond-woman" (Gen. 21:10), hardly a term of endearment. The Lord uses the same term in speaking to Abraham about Ishmael (v. 13). Therefore, Ishmael never seems to have been elevated to the status of an heir.

In Sarai's eighty-ninth year, the Lord reminded Abram of the covenant made at Haran, that Abram's seed would be God's covenant people. At this subsequent visit, God established circumcision as the token of the covenant between God and Abraham. Abraham laughed, for God told him Sarah would have a son of her own (v. 16). But then he remembered that Ishmael might be designated her legal offspring and said,

"O that Ishmael might live before thee!" (v. 18). But God again corrected him: Sarah truly would have a son, Abraham should call his name Isaac ("laughter"), and the covenant would continue through him (v. 21). The ninety-nine-year-old Abraham circumcised every male in the household, including himself and thirteen-year-old Ishmael that same day but apparently did not tell Sarah about the promised son.

Sarah must have suffered greatly over the years and felt mocked of God. On numerous occasions God had promised her husband that he would be the father of nations and yet she, his wife, after more than seventy years of marriage had borne him no son. Then about three months later, the Lord, in company of two others (Gen. 18:1-15), visited Abraham and again promised him a son by Sarah, who overheard and laughed, "After I am waxed old shall I have pleasure, my lord being old also?" (v. 12). The Lord turned to Abraham and asked him why Sarah laughed: "Is anything too hard for the Lord?" (v. 14). Then the Lord promised to return in nine months when Sarah gave birth to her child.

Isaac was born at the appointed time and was circumcised on the eighth day. Commenting happily on his name, Sarah said, "God hath made me to laugh, so that all that hear will laugh with me" (Gen. 21:6). It was indeed an astonishing joke: a woman giving birth at age eighty-nine or ninety (17:17).

Sarah had finally provided her husband with an heir. Isaac was the firstborn son of Abraham's chief wife and had full rights of heirship, taking precedence over an adoptive son or the son of a slave-wife. But about the time of Isaac's weaning, Sarah found Ishmael mocking Isaac (Gen. 21:9). Sarah demanded that Abraham expel Hagar and her son. As owner of the slave, Sarah still had control over Hagar and Ishmael. She had given her to Abraham—and she could take her away, compelling Abraham to divorce her (i.e., cast her out of his house). Abraham reluctantly (v. 11) divorced Hagar and sent her and her son away with nothing but bread and water.

Hagar

Hagar, apparently through no choice of her own, was the slave-wife of Abraham. There is no evidence that she was a reluctant wife. Through their son Ishmael, Abraham fathered the Arabs. Through Sarah's son Isaac, Abraham fathered the Hebrews. Through his wife Keturah, Abraham fathered the Midianites, the Kenites, and other nations. Hagar has the dubious distinction of being the only woman in the narratives to be divorced by her patriarch/husband.

Hagar was a tragic figure. She apparently first joined Abram's entourage in Egypt, where she is identified as "an handmaid [or slave], an Egyptian" (Gen. 16:1). This suggests that she was Pharaoh's personal gift to Sarai.

Of all the types of slaves, what sort was Hagar? Most ancient Near Eastern legal documents describe slavery as an accepted institution.[27] Although no Egyptian legal code is extant, Egyptian documents, correspondence, and stories from earliest times on the subject of slavery are in accord with other contemporary legal systems.

Though there were differences in the laws about male and female slaves, the source of slavery was the same. The earliest slaves were prisoners of war, designated as booty. Later, most became slaves as the result of insolvency. Interest rates were not limited by law and ranged from 20-33 percent. A debtor could pledge his property, himself, his wife, his children, or any combination. If a debtor was unable to pay, the creditor could seize all secured collateral without reprieve and sell the debtors, individually or collectively.[28]

There was also a brisk foreign slave trade.[29] Like captive slaves, they were permanent slaves in contrast to debtor slaves who had to be released after a time period. Houseborn slaves were those born into slavery in the household, either to paired slaves or to female slaves and family members such as the master or his sons. The mothers of such houseborn slaves were generally of foreign birth unless they had been sold into permanent slavery as children. The children were usually better treated and more trusted than purchased slaves and were considered sons or daughters of the household.[30]

According to the Mosaic code, thieves who could not restore the stolen property plus a penalty, could be sold by the victims into slavery (Ex. 22:3). Other sources of slaves throughout the ancient Near East included sale of self, sale of minor children, and adoption of freeborn children.[31] A man who could not find work or was heavily in debt and unable to extricate himself could sell first his children and then himself and his wife into slavery.[32]

Because Hagar was Egyptian, she could be neither a captive slave[33] nor an imported slave, or she would have been freed in Egypt. Slaves sold for insolvency served for specified periods of time, such as three years under the Code of Hammurabi or six years under the Mosaic code.[34] Because Hagar was a slave owned by the royal family, she could not have been an adopted daughter. Therefore, she was either an Egyptian child sold by her parents into permanent slavery or a houseborn slave of Egyptian parentage.[35]

If she was such a permanent slave, Hagar was a chattel that could be bought, sold, leased, exchanged, pledged, gifted, or inherited.[36] Permanent slaves were chattels or personal property, and no family records were kept for them.[37]

It is not known whether Hagar's mistress had other slaves, but Abram owned many.[38] All these slaves were his property, and if he had chosen a handmaid from among his own slaves, he would have controlled title to the children. When Abram accepted Hagar, Sarai's maid, any children born of this coupling would be under Sarai's control.[39]

However, not only ownership and control of personal property but also hierarchical authority was an issue in this situation. Sarai was chief wife or matriarch, but Abram was the patriarch and as such was the leader of the family or clan under his jurisdiction. As the patriarch he would be consulted on all important matters affecting the family, and all property of the family came under his control. Still he could not interfere with his wife's dowry or slaves.[40] Because of Abram's patriarchal authority, it was not improper for the Lord in speaking to Abram about his second wife to refer to Hagar as "thy bondwoman" (Gen. 21:12). In other instances, she is referred to as belonging to Sarai (16:1-6, 8, 9; 25:12). However, when Sarah comes the last time to demand that Hagar be cast out along with her son, she expresses no possessiveness for she calls Hagar "this bondwoman" twice (21:10) and asserts, "for the son of this bondwoman shall not be heir with my son" (21:10).

Although Hagar probably had no choice in the arrangement, she could look forward to her freedom upon divorce or upon Abraham's death, if Abraham's culture were governed by the contemporary laws of Old Babylon.[41]

We know little about the formalities of slave-wife marriages, but they required at minimum: (1) an arrangement provided by the chief wife where she asked her husband to take her maid to wife; (2) intent on the part of the three parties to obtain children by the arrangement to serve as possible heirs of the husband; and (3) consummation.

When Sarai offered Hagar to Abram, she took the initiative. There was no bride-price, no dowry, no bride-gift, and no contract, only intent and consummation, for Abram "went in unto Hagar, and she conceived" (Gen. 16:4). Her conception brought more grief than solace to all the parties.

When Hagar later fled into the wilderness, the angel who appeared to her addressed her as "Hagar, Sarai's maid." In

87

responding to his question about what she was doing, Hagar acknowledged that she was fleeing from "my mistress Sarai." The angel instructed her to "return to thy mistress and submit thyself under her hands" (Gen. 16:8-9). Neither of them mentions Abram. Instead the issue is clearly Hagar's relationship to Sarai.

Although Hagar returned, reconciled herself to Sarai, and gave birth to Ishmael, Sarai did not accept Ishmael as her firstborn. Thus Ishmael remained legally and biologically the son of Hagar. Children shared their mother's status. Hagar was a secondary wife, so Ishmael was a secondary son, even though he was heir apparent. Ishmael would be Abram's primary heir if (1) Abram had no biological sons by Sarai; (2) if Sarai acknowledged Ishmael as her son, thereby elevating him from secondary to primary son status as her legal son; or (3) if after Sarah's death, Abraham did not marry another chief wife and have sons.

On the basis of Genesis 21:11, it could be argued that Abraham did acknowledge Ishmael, son of Hagar, as his son[42] and therefore as an heir: "And the thing was very grievous in Abraham's sight *because of his son*" (italics added). But Abraham did not have standing to enfranchise Ishmael. According to the contemporary code of Hammurabi (and the later Middle Assyrian law), if he had had sons by his own slave-wife, he could have enfranchised them,[43] but he had no jurisdiction over Ishmael as long as Sarah was alive. Only she could enfranchise Ishmael.

Slave-wives such as Hagar and their children were slaves until their masters died, they were divorced, or they were freed by an act of manumission. Manumitted slaves usually received a legal document verifying their freedom.[44]

Hagar had no more children. Considering the ease with which she became pregnant, it is safe to assume that Sarah did not permit her to return to her husband's connubial bed after the birth of Ishmael. Hagar still would have taken great comfort in her status, for she had a son she assumed would be the sole heir of her wealthy and powerful husband. If Sarah died before Abraham, Hagar would be his concubine and senior wife unless he married another chief wife. If Abraham died before Sarah, Ishmael would be the heir and patriarch, and Hagar, his biological mother, would be free and would have a position of importance in the clan even though Ishmael would be the legal son of Sarah. All Hagar's future expectations were dashed when she heard that her eighty-nine-year-old mistress was pregnant. It must have been a tremendous shock and a source of considerable grief to her. Her world collapsed even more around her the day Sarah found Ishmael mocking Isaac (Gen. 21:9).

Was Abraham justified in divorcing Hagar? Jesus later said, "Moses because of the hardness of your hearts suffered you to put away your wives: but from the beginning it was not so" (Matt. 19:8). Was he referring to some ancient legal system that prohibited divorce? The oldest laws extant come from the ancient Near East. Was there a time when a Near Eastern legal system forbade divorce?

The oldest written law, the Code of Ur-Nammu dating from the twenty-fourth century B.C., allowed divorce but, like all the codes until the time of Hammurabi, made divorce a male privilege and did not formally recognize cases or grounds for divorce initiated by the wife. The Code of Ur-Nammu required that a husband initiating a divorce pay his wife one mina (sixty shekels) of silver. This was an expensive penalty (about six years salary for a common shepherd) to discourage divorce.[45]

Sumerian laws, incomplete as they are, do not mention divorce, although a twentieth-century B.C. Sumerian divorce settlement recorded in the city of Ur gave the wife ten shekels of silver, and she relinquished any other claims she had against her husband.[46]

89

The next oldest code, the Laws of Eshnunna dating from about the twentieth century, contained an even more rigorous penalty against divorce. If a husband wished to divorce his wife who had borne him children, he was cast out of his home and lost all his possessions.[47]

The Code of Lipit-Ishtar, dating from about the nineteenth century B.C., is unclear. No statute speaks specifically of divorce. Section 28 refers to a husband who "has turned his face away from his first wife," but this does not appear to be a divorce. It seems to be a change in the original intent of their marriage. The context makes it apparent that the wife has and will remain in his house and that he must continue to support her, in his home if she wishes, if he remarries.[48]

Hammurabi in the eighteenth century B.C. reinstated some of the severity of the Laws of Eshnunna by requiring the husband upon divorce to return his wife's dowry in full and give her one-half of his estate if she had borne sons.[49] If she were childless or perhaps had only daughters, he had to return her dowry and pay a cash penalty equal to his original bride-price.[50]

A court case recorded at Larsa during the reign of Rim-Sin, a monarch Hammurabi defeated, requires the divorcing husband to provide his wife with "a food and clothing allowance"—the equivalent of modern alimony.[51]

Hammurabi's code is also the first to address the question of a wife seeking a divorce. If she was deemed innocent of fault, she was free to take her dowry and leave. If she was at fault, however, she would be drowned, a severe penalty against women that had no counterpart in the divorce laws for men.[52]

Old Babylonian marriage contracts dating from about the nineteenth to the seventeenth centuries B.C. follow a fairly standard format, but the divorce penalty is variable. For example, a marriage contract from Nippur provided that if the husband wished to divorce his wife—a procedure requiring him to pronounce the words "You are not my wife"—he would have to return her nineteen-shekel dowry and pay her one-half mina of silver (thirty shekels) as her divorce-money.[53] The contract also provided that if she wished to divorce him by saying, "You are not my husband," she would be required to forfeit her dowry and pay him a half mina of silver, but this was apparently a fine since the contract does not specify the sum as "divorce-money."

In one unique marriage contract from this same region and period, if the wife wanted to divorce her husband, he could shave her and sell her as a slave. But she had a similar right. If he decided to divorce her, she could shave him, keep him as her slave, and require him to provide her with minimum amounts of wool and oil.[54]

However, these two contracts, which offer significant protection to women in the case of divorce, were atypical. More typically the husband had to pay a cash penalty for divorcing his wife, but the wife risked paying with her life—being either drowned or thrown from a tower.[55]

By the time of the Middle Assyrian Empire during approximately the fourteenth century B.C., laws offered women less protection. Here a husband was allowed to eject his wife from his home with or without money, as he chose.[56] Further if a husband abandoned a wife or disappeared without a trace, she had to wait a minimum of five years before she could remarry—and if she had sons who could support her, she could never remarry.[57]

The Hittite law from about the thirteenth century B.C. near the time of Moses is damaged and incomplete. But the statutes available suggest that a husband could divorce his wife by selling her for twelve shekels of silver.[58] This price was below the price of a slave and may have applied only if she had been guilty of illicit behavior. This law also permits a wife to divorce her husband, but the statute is incomplete and the terms are

91

missing. They suggest that the wife had to pay the husband something and that he got custody of the children.[59]

The laws of Moses also permitted divorce. The key statute is found in Deuteronomy 24:1: "When a man hath taken a wife, and married her, and it come to pass that she find no favour in his eyes, because he hath found some uncleanness in her: then let him write her a bill of divorcement, and give it in her hand, and send her out of his house." This is the first ancient code requiring the husband to find cause for the divorce. It is unfortunate that the cause is defined only as "some uncleanness," a phrase that may have had more precise connotations in the past than it currently does.

The Hebrew for "some uncleanness" is *erwat davar*, variously translated as "shameful exposure (of genitals), indecency, improper behavior, an unclean or unseemly thing".[60] The word thus seems to cover a broad range of behavior. Adultery has been universally accepted as "some uncleanness," but what of lesser faults and blemishes? Isaiah said that the Lord had divorced Israel for iniquity (Isa. 50:1), which included perversion, idolatry, and adultery.[61] Thus despite the vagueness of the term, the Mosaic code defines serious moral transgressions as "maximum" grounds for divorce but does not clearly communicate the "minimum" grounds.

The Old Testament, however, mentions two situations in which divorce was strictly prohibited. In the first case a bridegroom could accuse his bride of not being a virgin and arraign her before the elders of the city. If the wife's parents were able to prove her virginity by producing the bloodstained cloth from her matrimonial bed, then the husband had to pay the father a double bride-price of one hundred shekels of silver and was prohibited from ever divorcing her (Deut. 22:13-21).

The second case involved the rape of a virgin. If she was betrothed, the rapist was killed. If she was not betrothed, he was required to pay her father a fine equal to the bride-price of fifty shekels. He was then required to marry her unless her father refused (Ex. 22:17) and was not permitted ever to divorce her (Deut. 22:28-29).

The Middle Assyrian laws had an almost identical statute, which required the offended father to force the rapist's wife into prostitution.[62] Families were responsible for the actions of their members: if a woman of one family suffered, a woman of the offending family had to suffer also.

An interesting legal statute is Exodus 21:7-11, which has generated less comment than it warrants. This statute permits a father to sell his daughter as a concubine (Exodus uses the term "wife") to the master of the house or to one of his sons. Upon marriage she has all the legal rights of marriage, including maintenance, protection, and the right to bear children. If her husband were to marry a second wife, who would probably be a chief wife since the first was a concubine, he could not reduce the first's food, clothing, or duty of marriage. If he did so the concubine could divorce him. Under the Mosaic code then some women had legal rights of divorce for cause, but the cause appears to be limited to denial of support or conjugal relations.

Early Jewish law dating from the third through the seventh centuries A.D. permitted a husband to divorce easily and return the wife's dowry to her. He was required to show cause, but causes could be as trivial as burning his supper or finding a more attractive woman.[63] More serious causes involved violations of religious ritual such as serving him untithed food or having sexual relations with him during her period. For these causes he could divorce her without returning her dowry.[64]

No known ancient legal code denied men the right to divorce. With the exception of the Mosaic code and Jewish law, no ancient legal system required the husband to show cause for the divorce. On the other hand in the few instances where the wife was allowed to divorce, she was required to show cause such as abandonment or a relationship in which she has been grievously belittled by a cheating husband. If she could not show cause but was found instead to be belittling her husband, he was free to marry another woman and make his first wife a slave in his household.[65]

The earliest codes prescribed severe economic penalties for husbands who cast out the mothers of their children, but later codes, altered by male jurists, moderated these penalties until men could divorce their wives with little or no obstacle.

What then was Jesus referring to when he said, "From the beginning it was not so"? Malachi, writing about the fifth century B.C., asserted, "For the Lord, the God of Israel, saith that he hateth putting away [divorce]" (Mal. 2:16). At this period, the Israelite practice had developed of men divorcing their wives simply to marry younger women.[66] Perhaps in saying "from the beginning," Jesus was referring to Adam and Eve as an ideal marriage—a marriage in which God participated. Jesus would have us understand that if God is involved in a marriage, divorce has no place in it (Mark 9:10). The secular laws of divorce do not apply to those who are married and become "one flesh" in God.

What then of Abraham? The laws of his day permitted divorce without cause. But Abraham was prophet and patriarch. As God was involved in his life, he was also involved in his marriages. God confirmed Abraham's marriage to Sarah at least in their later years, if not before. By promising them a future son, God clearly assumed the continuation of their union.

When Hagar fled into the desert from the wrath of Sarai and was met there by the angel, she was told to return and submit to her mistress. Because the angel simultaneously ratified the marriage of Abraham and Hagar and the mistress/slave relationship between Sarah and Hagar by telling

Hagar to return, God was also involved in this three-way marriage.

When Isaac was born and Ishmael mocked him, Sarah, as chief wife and matriarch, demanded that Abraham cast out Hagar and Ishmael. Abraham was reluctant to do so. God intervened: "Let it not be grievous in thy sight because of the lad, and because of thy bondwoman; in all that Sarah hath said unto thee, hearken unto her voice; for in Isaac shall thy seed be called" (Gen. 21:11-12).

Probably the most comforting statement was God's assurance to Abraham, "Of the son of the bondwoman will I make a nation, because he is thy seed" (Gen. 21:13). This ostensibly confirmed Sarah's stewardship over the slave-wife and her son, including her right to punish them. While God had earlier ratified Abraham's marriage to Hagar, he now ratified their divorce. Therefore their divorce was not of men but of God.

But there was prejudice at least against a man divorcing his concubine if she had borne him children or casting out the children of such a concubine. For example, a Nuzi marriage contract of the thirteenth century B.C. required the bride to provide a slave for her husband should she prove barren. The contract further stipulated that the wife could not send these children away.[67] This contract may have been both typical and traditional, or it may have reflected an individual case of a husband trying to prevent his wife from exercising her traditional prerogative of sending away the children of the slave-wife if she became dissatisfied with them.

Now what about Sarah? Was she justified in casting out Hagar? In an Old Assyrian marriage contract that probably predates Abraham, we find: "Laqipum took (in marriage) Hatale, the daughter of Enishru. In the country Laqipum shall not take (in marriage) another (woman), (but) in the city (of Ashshur) he may take (in marriage) a qadistum [hierodule]. If within 2 years she [Hatale] has not procured offspring for him, only she may buy a maid-servant and even later on, *after she procures somehow an infant for him, she may sell her [the bearer of the child] where(soever) she pleases.* If Laqipum divorces her, he will pay 5 minas of silver, and if Hatale divorces him, she will pay 5 minas of silver" (italics added).[68] As this contract shows, the wife had continuous and exclusive control over the slave-wife and her offspring and could sell the slave-wife even if the slave-wife had borne a child. The wife's authority extended over the child or children of the slave-wife, but if they too were sent away, the husband's recourse was to marry a second wife.[69]

This custom was still practiced more than a millennium later and documented in a Neo-Assyrian marriage contract from the mid-first millennium B.C.: "If Subetu does not conceive (and) does not give birth, she may take a maidservant (and) as a substitute in her position she may place (her). She (Subetu) will (thereby) bring sons into being (and) the sons will be her (Subetu's) sons. If she loves (the maidservant) she may keep (her). If she hates (her) she may sell her."[70] Where the wife provided her husband with a slave to bear children, she generally retained control over the slave. The contract also affirms that the children of the maidservant belonged to Subetu.

In the context of ancient law, assuming Sarah was applying such a consideration, she had three choices: (1) free Hagar and send her away (universal law); (2) put the mark of a slave on her and reduce her to servitude with the other slaves (Babylonian law); or (3) punish her (Sumerian Law).[71] Perhaps because she was neither vengeful nor hardhearted, Sarah chose to free her, permitting Abraham to send her away.

Thus Abraham did not intervene. "And Abraham rose up early in the morning, and took bread, and a bottle of water, and gave it unto Hagar, putting it on her shoulder, and the child, and sent her away" (Gen. 21:14). Many statutes govern-

96

ing divorce from the time of Hammurabi and earlier, required cash settlements on the part of the husband. No statutes mandate the payment of settlement on the part of a wife who has her slave sent away, even where the slave bore children. Hagar brought nothing to the marriage, and Sarah required that she take nothing with her when she left. As for Ishmael, "God was with the lad; and he grew, and dwelt in the wilderness, and became an archer" (v. 20). Hagar and Ishmael settled in the wilderness of Paran (v. 21) in south-central Sinai. Hagar found an Egyptian wife for Ishmael, and his descendants became some of the great Arab nations.

Keturah

Little is known of Keturah. We do not even know when she married Abraham, though the positioning of her account seems to suggest it was after the death of Sarai. We do know she was fertile, where Sarai was not. Also she was much younger than Abraham. He was 147 when Sarai died, and he married Keturah when she was still young enough to bear six sons. Finally Keturah's marriage was not as a chief wife but as a concubine.[72]

Presumably Sarai provided the primary reason for Abraham's marrying Keturah as a concubine. Sons of secondary wives—concubines and slave-wives—were not heirs of their fathers under any known ancient legal code,[73] although they were heirs of their mother's estates. Unfortunately, secondary wives rarely had meaningful estates.[74]

If they were not declared sons during the father's lifetime, sons of slave-wives were freed upon his death. Such sons followed the status of their mothers—if she was free, so were they; if she remained a slave, so did they.[75]

None of Keturah's sons became heirs. They were secondary sons and never elevated to the status of heirs. It was not necessary to grant the sons of Keturah freedom as in the case of Ishmael, because they were already free. Abraham gave them gifts or money with which to establish their financial independence. In so doing Abraham did more than the law required and yet kept his commitment with God and Sarah that Isaac would be his only heir (Gen. 21:12).[76]

The sons of Keturah included Midian, the forebearer of Zipporah, wife of Moses.

Notes

1. Prior to the birth of Isaac, Abraham's name was Abram and Sarai's name was Sarai. When God promised them a son, he changed their names presumably to reflect their new status. Abraham means "father of nations" and Sarai means "princess" (Gen. 17:5, 15).

2. Josephus, "Antiquities of the Jews," in *Josephus: Complete Works*, trans. William Whiston (1960; rprt. Grand Rapids: Kregel Publications, 1972), 32.

3. E. A. Speiser, *Oriental and Biblical Studies: Collected Writings of E. A. Speiser*, eds. J. J. Finkelstein and Moshe Greenburg (Philadelphia: University of Pennsylvania Press, 1967), 76.

4. "The Story of Two Brothers," in James B. Pritchard, ed., *Ancient Near Eastern Texts* (Princeton, NJ: Princeton University Press, 1969), 23-25.

5. Middle Assyrian Law A 22: "If in the case of a seignior's wife one not her father, nor her brother, nor her son, but another person, has caused her to take to the road, but he did not know that she was a seignior's wife, he shall (so) swear and he shall also pay two talents of lead to the woman's husband. If [he knew that she was a seignior's wife], he shall pay the damages [and swear], 'I never lay with her.' However, if the [seignior's] wife [has declared], 'He did lie with me,' when the man has paid the damages to the seignior, he shall go [to the] river, although he had no (such) agreement; if he has turned back from the river, they shall treat him as the woman's husband treated his wife"; ibid., 181.

6. Josephus, "Antiquities of the Jews," 33. Mathematics as understood by the Old Babylonian/Sumerian scholars was at least as sophisticated as that known by the Greeks centuries later.

7. If Eliezer's adoption contract with Abraham was typical of the times, it would have addressed the possibility of a son being born to Abraham. Such contracts did not usually completely disinherit the adopted son. Yet if this Eliezer was the same trusted servant who was called more than fifty-three years later to go to Padanaram and obtain a wife for Isaac, he informed the family at Padanaram that "unto him [Isaac] hath he [Abraham] given all that he hath" (Gen. 24:36). Either Abraham's contract with Eliezer allowed him to remove the servant as heir in the event a son was born, or Abraham was able to send him away before this time with gifts as he did for his sons by Keturah. Or perhaps Eliezer died in the intervening years, rendering the problem moot.

8. Thomas E. McComiskey, "The Status of the Secondary Wife: Its Development in Ancient Near Eastern Law. A Study and Comprehensive Index," Ph.D. diss., Brandeis University, 1965, 59.

9. In my opinion, one of the most heart-wrenching scenarios in the Old Testament is the story of Sarai. Her husband Abraham was a visionary man, and it seems each message from God included a promise that her husband would be the father of nations (Gen. 12:2). Sarai must have spent much time contemplating her options. Nothing would have been more on her mind.

10. "If the man, who has taken the infant in adoption to himself and has brought him up, has built him a house (and) afterwards gets sons and sets his face to expel the adopted child, that son shall not then go destitute; the father who has brought him up shall give him one-third of his inheritance out of his property when he goes; (but) he shall not give him any (portion) of field plantation or house." Code of Hammurabi 191, in G. R. Driver and J. C. Miles, eds., The Babylonian Laws, 2 vols. (Oxford: Oxford University Press, 1968), 2:75. See also David Neiman, "Patriarchal Institutions," Ph.D. diss., Dropsie College, 1955, 67.

11. The advantage for the wife of such an arrangement—assuming that the alternative was for the husband to acquire a second wife

of equal status—was that the wife remained in control of the slave as long as her husband lived and, if she wished, of the slave's child. Although Hagar had no say, such an arrangement would also be to her advantage, for she became a legal wife (slave-wife) of Abram, though she continued as a slave to Sarai. This meant that she would automatically be free upon divorce or Abram's death. There was no bride-price, no dowry, no bride-gift, and no contract, only intent and consummation, for Abram "went in unto Hagar, and she conceived" (Gen. 16:4).

12. Driver and Miles, *The Babylonian Laws*, 1:305.

13. Reuven Yaron, *Introduction to the Law of the Aramaic Papyri* (Oxford: Clarendon Press, 1961), 36.

14. Code of Hammurabi 145, 146, in Pritchard, *Ancient Near Eastern Texts*, 172.

15. Raymond Westbrook, "Old Babylonian Marriage Law," Ph.D. diss., University of Michigan, Ann Arbor, 1982, 134.

16. Louis M. Epstein, *Marriage Laws in the Bible and Talmud* (1942; rprt. New York: Johnson Reprint Corporation, 1968), 50.

17. Gen. 21:14; Code of Hammurabi 171, in Driver and Miles, *The Babylonian Laws*, 2:67.

18. Yaron, *Introduction to the Law*, 38, 39.

19. "If a man has died (and) his veiled wife has no sons, the sons of concubines(?) (become his) sons; they shall take a share (of his property)." Middle Assyrian Law A 41, in G. R. Driver and J. C. Miles, eds., *The Assyrian Laws* (Oxford: Clarendon Press, 1935), 411.

20. "If a man has married a priestess and she has given a slave-girl to her husband and she bears sons, (if) thereafter that slave-girl goes about making herself equal to her mistress, because she has borne sons her mistress shall not sell her; she may put the mark (of a slave) on her and may count her with the slave-girls." Code of Hammurabi 146, in Driver and Miles, *The Babylonian Laws*, 2:57.

21. "If she has not borne sons, her mistress may sell her." Code of Hammurabi 147, in ibid., 2:57.

22. "If a man's slave-woman, comparing herself to her mistress,

100

speaks insolently to her, her mouth shall be scoured with 1 quart of salt." Laws of Ur-Nammu 22, in Pritchard, *Ancient Near Eastern Texts*, 525.

23. "If a man's wife has not borne him children but a harlot (from) the public square has borne him children, he shall provide grain, oil and clothing for that harlot; the children which the harlot has borne him shall be his heirs, and as long as his wife lives, the harlot shall not live in the house with the wife." Code of Lipit-Ishtar 27, in Francis Rue Steele, "The Code of Lipit-Ishtar," *American Journal of Archaeology* 52 (1948): 442.

24. "If a man has died (and) his veiled wife has no sons, the sons of concubines (become his) sons; they shall take a share (of his property)." Middle Assyrian Law A 41, in Driver and Miles, *The Assyrian Laws*, 409.

25. "If the first wife of a man has borne him sons and his slave-girl has borne him sons, (and) the father in his life-time states to the sons whom the slave-girl has borne him '(You are) my sons', he shall count them with the sons of the first wife and the sons of the slave-girl shall take proportionate shares in the property of the paternal estate; an heir, (being) a son of the first wife, shall choose and take the first share at the division." Code of Hammurabi 170, in Driver and Miles, *The Babylonian Laws*, 2: 65.

26. Gen. 21:11; Tikva Frymer-Kensky, "Patriarchal Family Relationships and Near Eastern Law," *The Biblical Archeologist* 44 (Fall 1981): 213.

27. Isaac Mendelsohn, *Slavery in the Ancient Near East: A Comparative Study of Slavery in Babylonia, Assyria, Syria, and Palestine from the Middle of the Third Millennium to the End of the First Millennium* (Westport, CT: Greenwood Press, 1978), 1.

28. Ibid., 23, 26.

29. Ibid., 3.

30. Ibid., 57.

31. Adoption was a common business practice in most of the ancient codes. A parent could sell a son or a daughter to an adoptive parent. The selling parents received cash and also did not have to provide for that child from their own estate. The adopted son or

daughter was essentially a slave until the adoptive parent died but then inherited a share or all of the estate. In this way adoptive parents could obtain cheap labor and security for their old age; the adopted slave would take care of them for life and give them a proper funeral to assist them in their life after death. Similarly, the adopted child had the advantage of an inheritance; ibid., 21.

32. Ibid., 15.

33. Hebrew law is unique in that no other code deals with the question of fair treatment for women captured in war. Like all soldiers, a Hebrew soldier had the right to take captives. If his captives included "a beautiful woman," he could make her his concubine and could not sell her (she was free), though he could divorce her (Deut. 21:10-14). The King James Version uses the term "thy wife"; but lacking contract or bride-price, her status would be that of a concubine.

34. "If a man has become liable to arrest under a bond and has sold his wife his son or his daughter or gives (them) into servitude, for 3 years they shall do work in the house of him who has bought them or taken them in servitude; in the fourth year their release shall be granted." Code of Hammurabi 117, in Driver and Miles, *The Babylonian Laws*, 2:47.

"And if thy brother, an Hebrew man, or an Hebrew woman, be sold unto thee, and serve thee six years; then in the seventh year thou shalt let him go free from thee." Deut. 15:12.

35. Female slaves were the chattels or personal property of their owners. Unauthorized sexual use or rape of a slave was deemed a theft of property from the owner. If the owner was a woman, her husband had sexual rights only with her permission. If a female slave was a chattel of a male owner, he had full sexual rights and could extend those rights to anyone he chose, such as sons, friends, or guests. It was also common to pair her with a male slave. Any children born to a female slave had their mother's status, regardless of who fathered the child. The child became a slave of the estate or a household slave.

36. Mendelsohn, *Slavery in the Ancient Near East*, 34.

37. C. H. W. Johns, *The Relations Between the Laws of Babylonia*

and *The Laws of the Hebrew Peoples* (London: Oxford University Press, 1914), 12.

38. Abraham pursued the captors of Lot and his family with 318 "trained servants, born in his own house" (Gen. 14:14). The Hebrew word for trained servant is *"hanik."* This may mean "armed retainer"; R. L. Harris, G. L. Archer, Jr., and B. K. Waltke, eds. *Theological Wordbook of the Old Testament* (Chicago: Moody Press, 1980), 301. Or "his tried and trusty men"; William Gesenius, *A Hebrew and English Lexicon of the Old Testament* ed. F. Brown, S. R. Driver, and C. A. Briggs (Oxford: Clarendon Press, 1976), 335. Presumably the reference to being born in his own house leads Keil and Delitzsch to label these men slaves; see C. F. Keil and F. Delitzsch, *Commentary on the Old Testament in Ten Volumes* (Grand Rapids, MI: William B. Eerdmans Publishing Company, 1985), 1:205. We know that Abraham had many maidservants (Gen. 12:16) and, in addition to those born in his house, other slaves purchased with money (17:13).

39. Compare Code of Hammurabi 146-47, in Pritchard, *Ancient Near Eastern Texts*, 172, with Code of Hammurabi 170-71, in ibid., 173.

40. Driver and Miles, *The Babylonian Laws*, 1:272.

41. "However, if the father during his lifetime has never said 'My children!' to the children whom the slave bore him, after the father has gone to (his) fate, the children of the slave may not share in the goods of the paternal estate along with the children of the first wife; freedom for the slave and her children shall be effected, with the children of the first wife having no claim at all against the children of the slave for service. . . ." Code of Hammurabi 171, in Pritchard, *Ancient Near Eastern Texts*, 173.

42. Frymer-Kensky, "Patriarchal Family Relationships," 213.

43. "If a man has died (and) his veiled wife has no sons, the sons of concubines(?) (become his) sons; they shall take a share (of his property)." Middle Assyrian Law A 41, in Driver and Miles, *The Assyrian Laws*, 409; Code of Hammurabi 170-71, in Driver and Miles, *The Babylonian Laws*, 2:65.

44. Freed slaves were generally regarded as second-class citizens. In fact Jewish law about twenty centuries later would place them at

the very bottom of hierarchal status, below bastards, temple slaves, and proselytes. See Horayoth 3.8, in Herbert Danby, trans., *The Mishna* (Oxford: Oxford University Press, 1985), 466.

45. "If a man divorces his primary wife, he must pay (her) one mina of silver." Laws of Ur-Nammu 6, in Pritchard, *Ancient Near Eastern Texts*, 524.

46. "Final judgment: Lu-Utu, the son of Nig-Baba, divorced Geme-Enlil. Dugidu, an officer and official took oath that Geme-Enlil had taken her stand (and) said, 'By the king! Give me 10 Shekels of silver (and) I will not enter claim against you,' (and) that she made him forfeit 10 shekels of silver." Pritchard, *Ancient Near Eastern Texts*, 217.

47. "If a man divorces his wife after having made her bear children and takes [ano]ther wife, he shall be driven from his house and from whatever he owns and may go after him who will accept him." Laws of Eshnunna 59, in ibid., 163.

48. "If a man has turned his face away from his first wife. . . . but she has not gone out of the [house]; his wife which he married *as his favorite* is a second wife; he shall continue to support his first wife." Code of Lipit-Ishtar 28, in Steele, "The Code of Lipit-Ishtar," 442.

49. "If a man sets his face to divorce a lay-sister who has borne him sons or a priestess who has provided him with sons, they shall render her dowry to her and shall give her a half-portion of field plantation or chattels and she shall bring up her sons"; Code of Hammurabi 137, in Driver and Miles, *The Babylonian Laws*, 2:55.

50. "If a man wishes to divorce his first wife who has not borne him sons, he shall give her money to the value of her bridal gift and shall make good to her the dowry which she has brought from her father's house and (so) divorce her." Code of Hammurabi 138, in ibid.

51. Westbrook, "Old Babylonian Marriage Law," 1:292.

52. "If a woman has hated her husband and states 'Thou shalt not have (the natural use of) me,' the facts of her case shall be determined in her district and, if she has kept herself chaste and has no fault, while her husband is given to going about out (of doors)

104

and so has greatly belittled her, that woman shall suffer no punishment; she may take her dowry and goes to her father's house." Code of Hammurabi 142, in Driver and Miles, *The Babylonian Laws*, 2:57.

"If she has not kept herself chaste but is given to going about out (of doors), will waste her house (and) so belittle her husband, they shall cast that woman into the water." Code of Hammurabi 143, in ibid.

53. Westbrook, "Old Babylonian Marriage Law," 185.

54. Ibid., 182.

55. "And (if) Wara-Shamash says to his wives 'You are not my wives', he shall pay 1 mina of silver. And (if) they say to their husband Warad-Shamash 'You are not our husband', they will bind them and cast them into the river." Ibid., 206, also 162, 165, 208, 227.

56. "If a man divorces his wife, if (it is) his will, he shall give her something; if (it is) not his will, he shall not give her anything; she shall go forth empty." Middle Assyrian Law A 37, in Driver and Miles, *The Assyrian Laws*, 405.

57. "If a woman is still dwelling in her father's house or if her husband has made her to dwell apart and her husband has gone to the field(s) (and) has left her neither oil nor wool nor clothing nor food nor anything else and has had no provision(?) brought to her from the field(s), that woman shall remain faithful to her husband for five years (and) not go to dwell with an(other) husband. If she has sons (and) they hire themselves out and earn their own living, the woman shall respect her husband (and) shall not go to dwell with an(other) husband. If she has no sons, she shall respect her husband for five years; at the beginning of the sixth year she may go to dwell with the husband of her choice. Her husband on coming (back) shall not claim her; she is free for her later husband. If he has delayed beyond the term of five years (and) has not kept himself away of his own accord, (inasmuch as) either a brigand(?) has seized him and he has disappeared, or he has been seized as (if he were) a robber(?) and been delayed (in returning), on coming (back) he shall make a (formal) claim (and) give a woman equivalent to his wife; and (then) he shall take back his wife. Or, if the king has sent him to any other country (and) he has been delayed beyond the term of five

years, his wife shall respect him and shall not go to dwell with an(other) husband. But, if she has gone to dwell with an(other) husband before the end of five years and has borne children, her husband on coming (back) shall take her herself and also her children, because she has not respected the marriage-contract but has been married(!)." Middle Assyrian Law A 36, in Driver and Miles, *The Assyrian Laws*, 403-405.

58. "If a man divorces a woman, and she . . . , he may sell her; whoever [buys her] shall give 12 shekels of silver." Hittite Law 26B, in Pritchard, *Ancient Near Eastern Texts*, 190.

59. "If a woman send away a man, she shall give him . . . and . . . The man shall get his children." Hittite Law 26A, in ibid.

60. Gesenius, *A Hebrew and English Lexicon*, 183, 789.

61. Harris, Archer, and Waltke, *Theological Wordbook*, 650.

62. "In the case of a seignior's [upper class freeman] daughter, a virgin who was living in her father's house, whose [father] had not been asked (for her in marriage), whose hymen had not been opened since she was not married, and no one had a claim against her father's house, if a seignior took the virgin by force and ravished her, either in the midst of the city or in the open country or at night in the street or in a granary or at a city festival, the father of the virgin shall take the wife of the virgin's ravisher and give her to be ravished; he shall not return her to her husband (but) take her; the father may give his daughter who was ravished to her ravisher in marriage. If he has no wife, the ravisher shall give the (extra) third in silver to her father as the value of a virgin (and) her ravisher shall marry her (and) not cast her off. If the father does not (so) wish, he shall receive the (extra) third for the virgin in silver (and) give his daughter to whom he wishes." Middle Assyrian Law 55, in Pritchard, *Ancient Near Eastern Texts*, 185.

63. "The School of Shammai say: A man may not divorce his wife unless he has found unchastity in her, for it is written, Because he hath found in her indecency in anything. And the school of Hillel say: [He may divorce her] even if she spoiled a dish for him, for it is written, Because he hath found in her indecency in anything. R. Akiba says: Even if he found another fairer than she, for it is written,

and it shall be if she find no favour in his eyes." Gittin 9.10, in Danby, *The Mishnah*, 321.

64. "These are they that are put away without their *Ketubah*: a wife that transgresses the Law of Moses and Jewish custom. What [conduct transgresses] the Law of Moses? If she gives her husband untithed food, or has connexion with him in her uncleanness, or does not set apart Dough-offering, or utters a vow and does not fulfil it. And what [conduct transgresses] Jewish custom? If she goes out with her hair unbound, or spins in the street, or speaks with any man. Abba Saul says: Also if she curses his parents in his presence. R. Tarfon says: Also [if she is] a scolding woman. And who is a scolding woman? Whosoever speaks inside her house so that her neighbours hear her voice." Ketuboth 7.6, in ibid., 255.

65. Code of Hammurabi 141: "If a married lady who is dwelling in a man's house sets her face to go out (of doors) and persists in behaving herself foolishly wasting her house (and) belittling her husband, they shall convict her and, if her husband then states that he will divorce her, he may divorce her; nothing shall be given to her (as) her divorce-money (on) her journey. If her husband states that he will not divorce her, her husband may marry another woman; that woman shall dwell as a slave-girl in the house of her husband." Driver and Miles, *The Babylonian Laws*, 2:55-57.

66. Adam Clarke, *The Holy Bible Containing the Old And New Testaments with a Commentary and Critical Notes* (Nashville: Abingdon Press, 1830), 802n14.

67. Cyrus H. Gordon, "Biblical Customs and the Nuzu Tablets," *The Biblical Archeologist* 3 (Feb. 1940): 3.

68. Julius Lewy, "On Some Institutions of the Old Assyrian Empire," *Hebrew Union College Annual* 27 (1956), 9-10; italics added.

69. Driver and Miles, *The Babylonian Laws*, 1:304.

70. A. K. Grayson and J. Van Seters, "The Childless Wife in Assyria and the Stories in Genesis," *Orientalia* 44 (1975): 485.

71. Laws of Ur-Nammu 22, in Pritchard, *Ancient Near Eastern Texts*, 525.

72. Gen. 25:6. In verse 1, Keturah is referred to as a "wife." A

concubine is a wife in every legal sense, except her status is below that of a chief wife. In verse 6, the word concubine is in the plural, perhaps including Hagar or suggesting that Abraham married at least two women after Sarai died although we know of no offspring other than those of Keturah.

73. "If a man married a wife and she bore him children and those children are living, and a slave also bore children for her master (but) the father granted freedom to the slave and her children, the children of the slave shall not divide the estate with the children of their (former) master." Code of Lipit-Ishtar 25, in Steele, "Code of Lipit-Ishtar," 441; see also Code of Hammurabi 171, in Driver and Miles, *The Babylonian Laws*, 2:67.

74. A man could also have sons by his own female slave—rather than a slave presented to him by his barren wife for the purpose of bearing children, who would be a slave-wife. While these sons were not automatically heirs, the codes favored their elevation to full sonship and so made it easy for them to become heirs. All the father had to do was declare sons of his female slaves or sons of his concubines "my sons" during his lifetime. Then they became full heirs. Code of Hammurabi 170, in Driver and Miles, *The Babylonian Laws*, 2:65.

75. Middle Assyrian laws dating from about 1400 B.C. added one clause in favor of sons of concubines and female slaves: if the father made no declaration during his lifetime and the first wife had no sons, the sons of the slave (concubine in the text) became his heirs (Middle Assyrian Law A 41, in Driver and Miles, *The Assyrian Laws*, 409). The sons of concubines and the sons of slave-wives that the wife provided to the husband were under her direction. If she accepted them as her own, they were heirs of her husband. If she did not receive them as her legal sons, they were not heirs and were accorded the same status as their mothers, i.e., they were secondary sons and obtained their freedom and nothing more, unless their mothers happened to have some assets. If that was the case, they were heirs of whatever estate she might have.

76. Abraham was father to four classes of sons. His oldest son was Eliezer, a servant or slave who became his son by adoption but

who was not biologically related to him. Next came Ishmael, his biological son by his slave-wife Hagar, who could have been also the "firstborn" son of his chief wife, Sarai, if Sarai had so designated him. She did not. Abraham's only son by his chief wife was Isaac. After Sarai died, Abraham had six sons by his concubine Keturah. Isaac clearly had the rights of the firstborn, and the others had lesser status determined by contract or the station of their mothers.

VI.

Rebekah's Household

Vivacious and outgoing Rebekah overshadowed Isaac, the quiet patriarch, whom she agreed to marry sight unseen. While pregnant she was told about her yet unborn children, Esau and Jacob. Certain that she had received the Lord's promise for Jacob, she intervened to ensure that Jacob obtained the firstborn blessing and birthright, even though he was secondborn, not stopping short of deception. Her story gives insight into bridal negotiations using an agent, and her bride-price and bride-gifts may have been some of the more extravagant on record.

Isaac's mother Sarah died at age 127. Three years later, when Isaac was forty, Abraham sent his most trusted servant to Haran to find a wife for Isaac from among relatives there. The servant loaded ten camels with goods and began his quest (Gen. 24:10).

At the well of Haran, the servant asked to be shown the maiden of his search and set up a specific scenario: he would ask for water from a maiden. If she gave him water and also watered his camels, she would be the Lord's chosen spouse for his young master. Rebekah arrived immediately and fulfilled the scenario in every respect. It was not an easy task to water ten thirsty camels, which consume enormous amounts of water. The servant paid her lavishly with an earring and bracelets weighing about ten and one-half shekels of gold or the equivalent of about ten years' wages—enough to buy five slaves at twenty silver shekels apiece.[1]

He then asked her name and if there was shelter in her father's house for himself and his camels. She answered, "I am the daughter of Bethuel, the son of Milcah, which she bare unto Nahor" (Gen. 24:24). Bethuel was a nephew of Abraham through his brother Nahor. Isaac and her father were first cousins, making Rebekah and Isaac first cousins once removed. This relationship was considered ideal for a marriage between propertied branches of the same family.

Rebekah offered Abraham's servant lodging and food for him and his men as well as food and accommodation for his camels. The servant then revealed his identity and his errand for Abraham. Rebekah ran home with the news. Her older brother Laban eyed Rebekah's gold bracelets and earring and raced out to the well. "Come in, thou blessed of the Lord," he said. "[W]herefore standest thou without? for I have prepared the house, and room for the camels" (Gen. 24:31). Even in his relative youth, Laban seemed to be an opportunist. As discussed in the previous chapter, he would further prove so in his dealings with Isaac and Rebekah's son, Jacob, and the bride-price for Leah and Rachel, Jacob's first cousins.

After attending to the camels, Laban invited everyone to eat. The servant may have been fasting on behalf of his errand, because he would not eat until he had negotiated on behalf of Isaac. He asked permission to return to Canaan with Rebekah as bride for Isaac. Laban and Bethuel, a younger brother (the father was dead),[2] agreed.

Genesis 24:53 and 55 specifically mention that Rebekah's mother helped make the decision and that she also received part of the bride-price. It seems likely that she helped with the

negotiations. Extant Old and Neo-Babylonian documents record cases where sons and mother negotiated wedding contracts for daughters.[3] The negotiators agreed to a contract, and
the servant gave Rebekah a princely bride-gift: "jewels of silver,
and jewels of gold, and raiment, and gave them to Rebekah:
he gave also to her brother and to her mother precious things"
(Gen. 24:53). The jewelry he had already given Rebekah
equalled more than three times the high average bride-price.[4]
For a dowry we know that Rebekah was given her nurse, who
accompanied her to Canaan (v. 59). (It was not uncommon
for the groom, through his agent, to give gifts to the bride's
family before the wedding. Such gifts were mostly food and
jewelry.[5])

As the caravan neared Abraham's home near Hebron,
Rebekah saw a man in a far field coming to meet them and
asked who it was. When she learned that it was Isaac, she
dismounted from the camel and went to meet him. Because
the contract had been negotiated, consideration paid, and
dowry received, Rebekah thus already had the status of the
chief wife, pending only the final consummation. Thereupon
"Isaac brought her into his mother Sarah's tent, and took
Rebekah, and she became his wife; and he loved her" (Gen.
24:67).

For twenty years Rebekah was unable to conceive. Isaac
approached God in prayer, and Rebekah conceived twins
(Gen. 25:21). These twins seemed to struggle in the womb,
and Rebekah asked God what this could mean. "And the Lord
said unto her, Two nations are in thy womb, and two manner
of people shall be separated from thy bowels; and the one
people shall be stronger than the other people; and the elder
shall serve the younger" (v. 23).

Although this communication could be variously inter-
preted, Rebekah believed it meant that Jacob should have the
firstborn birthright and blessing. But Isaac disagreed and

named Esau his firstborn. Esau, after all, fulfilled all the firstborn conventions discussed earlier: he was the chronological firstborn, he was the firstborn of the chief wife, and most importantly he was Isaac's favorite (Gen. 25:28).

Perhaps no twins have been less alike. The record allows us to form a picture of Esau as a burly, hairy, irresponsible, rough-and-tumble outdoorsman who constantly upset his mother—particularly when he married two Hittite women, Bathbeeri or Judith and Bashemath. But Isaac delighted in the meat that Esau provided for the table (Gen. 25:28).

Jacob in contrast was a gentle, smooth-skinned man who preferred to stay near home and tend the flocks (Gen. 25:27). He was Rebekah's favorite (v. 28). As Isaac grew old and blind (about 117 years old according to Adam Clarke),[6] Rebekah must have contemplated the prospects of her imminent widowhood. She was willing to deceive her husband to avoid being supported by Esau, possibly in the home of her two unliked daughters-in-law (27:46). She had a matriarchal responsibility for her sons and felt that God had directed her to ensure that the "elder shall serve the younger" (25:23).

Mothers in Israel did not nominate the firstborn son, but undoubtedly they were very interested and may have exerted great pressure on their husbands to nominate a certain son as firstborn. Rebekah must have made considerable effort to persuade Isaac to confer the firstborn blessing on Jacob. She finally plotted with Jacob to obtain the rights from Esau, apparently using the prophecy to justify deceitful and fraudulent behavior (Gen. 27:6-13). Jacob achieved this design in two steps.

In the first instance, Esau returned famished from a long and apparently unsuccessful hunt. Jacob had prepared a red lentil soup, which Esau wanted badly (Gen. 25:30). "Red," edom, is repeated in the Hebrew, accentuating the name by which Esau became known and for which he sold his birthright.[7] Jacob agreed to feed Esau in exchange for his birthright or the inheritance right which would give Esau two-thirds of Isaac's estate. Esau rationalized that his birthright would do him no good if he were dead of hunger and made the oath Jacob required: Esau "sware unto him: and he sold his birthright unto Jacob" (v. 33).

It is possible that the inheritance had little or no current value and Esau willingly sold it. We know that Jacob was penniless when he later fled from Esau (Gen. 28:20). Also the fact that Esau spent so much of his time hunting could suggest the possibility that the family was poor and that the wealth of Abraham had not continued in the family. It was not uncommon for desert marauders to swoop down on nomads and in a day strip them of all they had. Perhaps Isaac's inherited wealth had been lost and the property birthright was essentially worthless, leading Esau to "despise . . . his birthright" (25:34) and sell it.[8]

The second step in transferring the firstborn rights to Jacob occurred when Isaac felt he was about to die. He sent Esau out for some venison for his favorite stew before conferring upon him patrilineal rights of the firstborn, even though Esau's marriage to the Hittites was a "grief of mind unto Isaac" (Gen. 26:35).

Overhearing the conversation between Isaac and Esau, Rebekah quickly sent Jacob out to the flock to get a couple of young kids from which she made the stew Isaac loved. Then she dressed Jacob in Esau's clothes, covering his arms and neck with the skins of the kids, and sent him to Isaac, disguised as Esau, for his blessing.

The masquerade was not convincing. When he addressed Isaac as "my father," the old man asked, "Who art thou, my son?" When Jacob identified himself as Esau, Isaac asked how it was that he had returned so quickly from the hunt. Still suspicious Isaac felt his arms and smelled his raiment. Some doubts still lingered, for he observed, "The voice is Jacob's voice, but the hands are the hands of Esau" (Gen. 27:18-27). However, he was sufficiently convinced that he pronounced the blessing of leadership: "God give thee of the dew of heaven, and the fatness of the earth, and plenty of corn and wine: Let people serve thee, and nations bow down to thee: be lord over thy brethren, and let thy mother's sons bow down to thee: cursed be every one that curseth thee, and blessed be he that blesseth thee" (vv. 28-29). Isaac obviously thought that he was conferring upon Esau the leadership of the family since he mentions not only the recipient's supremacy but the subordination of "thy mother's sons."

When Esau returned from the hunt, made his savory stew, and presented himself to Isaac, he was stunned to find that Jacob had usurped his blessing. Weeping, he pled with his father for a blessing, but his father confirmed, "Behold, I have made him thy lord, and all his brethren have I given to him for servants; and with corn and wine have I sustained him: and what shall I do now unto thee, my son?" (Gen. 27:37)

No law allows one to benefit through fraud. But although Isaac was shocked and condemned Jacob (Gen. 27:35), Isaac did not retract the blessing. The most likely explanation is that he understood that the blessing rightly belonged to Jacob and that he had been wrong in attempting to bestow it on his favorite son.

After working for Laban in Padanaram, Jacob returned to Hebron with his wives and children. Isaac was still alive and lived approximately twenty-three more years.[9] Rebekah must have died, for she is not mentioned. When Isaac died both Esau and Jacob attended to the funeral rites. Then Esau returned to his home east of the Dead Sea in Edom (Gen. 36:8). Jacob, the son for whom Rebekah fought so hard, remained at his ancestral home in Hebron. This indicates that in accordance with his purchased firstborn birthright, he had inherited Isaac's lands. Similarly, in accordance with his firstborn blessing, Rebekah's favored son was the genealogical leader of the House of Israel. The chief characters of the Bible have been reckoned after Jacob, not after Esau.

Notes

1. Abraham's day preceded coinage. Common currency was in rings of bronze, silver, and occasionally gold. These rings were measured by weight, the most common of which was the shekel.

2. This would explain why Laban negotiates with Abraham's servant, why Rachel goes to her "mother's house" (v. 28), and why the bride-price is paid not only to Laban but also to Rebekah's unnamed mother (v. 53). See Josephus, "Antiquities of the Jews," in *Josephus: Complete Works*, trans. William Whiston (1960; rprt. Grand Rapids, MI: Kregel Publications, 1972), 38.

3. E. A. Speiser, *Oriental and Biblical Studies: Collected Writings of E. A. Speiser*, eds. J. J. Finkelstein and Moshe Greenburg (Philadelphia: University of Pennsylvania Press, 1967), 77.

4. See, for example, Barry L. Eichler, *Indenture at Nuzi: The Personal Tidennutu Contract and its Mesopotamian Analogues* (London: Yale University Press, 1973), 15.

5. Raymond Westerbrook, "Old Babylonian Marriage Law," *Archiv Für Orientforchung Beiheft* 23 (1988): 101.

6. Adam Clarke, *The Holy Bible Containing The Old and New Testaments with a Commentary and Critical Notes*, 4 vols. (Nashville, TN: Abingdon Press, 1830), 1:167.

7. Ibid., 160.

8. The sale of a birthright or an inheritance was not without precedent. A Nuzi contract records a transaction where one Tupkitilla sold his inheritance to his brother Kurpazah for three sheep: "On the day they divide the grove (that lies) on the road of the town of Lumti . . . , Tupkitilla shall give it to Kurpazah as his inheritance share. And Kurpazah has taken three sheep to Tupkitilla in exchange for his inheritance share." Cyrus H. Gordon, "Biblical Customs and

the Nuzu Tablets," *The Biblical Archeologist* 3 (Feb. 1940): 5; see also John Van Seters, *Abraham in History and Tradition* (New Haven, CT: Yale University Press, 1975), 93.

9. Clarke, *The Holy Bible*, 1:288.

VII.

POTIPHAR'S WIFE

Potiphar's wife played a small role in a larger drama. Her lust for her husband's slave Joseph traumatized him but led to beneficial consequences not only for the son of Rachel but the Egyptian commonwealth.

In Canaan prior to their meeting, Joseph was sold into slavery for twenty pieces of silver an average price for a seventeen-year-old boy at the time (Gen. 37:28).[1] The intended sellers were his exasperated brothers who were angered by their father's preferential treatment of him. But he was apprehended by Midianites who sold him to a caravan of Ishmaelites en route to Egypt before his brothers did. The Midianites were not professional slave traders; none are known during this period—about 1600-1500 B.C.—in the ancient world.

In Egypt the Ishmaelites sold Joseph for an undisclosed sum into permanent servitude as a foreign slave to Potiphar, an officer of Pharaoh.[2] Joseph prospered in Potiphar's service and became overseer of all that Potiphar had (Gen. 37:36; 39:1-6).

Trusted, capable slaves at this time were allowed to hold responsible positions and to own property. Some engaged in business, owned slaves, cattle, and land, appeared as bankers, and borrowed large amounts of money.[3] Potiphar trusted him so completely that he placed all he had in Joseph's hand, "and he {Potiphar} knew not aught he had, save the bread which he did eat" (Gen. 39:6). If ever a slave had expectations of a comfortable life, it was Joseph. His rise to leadership was spectacular, his fall from grace even more precipitous.

In addition to his managerial skills, Joseph was "goodly" and "well favoured" (Gen. 39:6). Potiphar's wife became infatuated with Joseph, but her sexual advances were refused (v. 7).

How could a slave refuse his mistress? First, of course, Potiphar's wife did not own Joseph. He had been bought by Potiphar, and just as Potiphar could not legally have sexual relations with a handmaid owned by his wife, neither could she have legal sexual relations with Joseph. The wife's rights to command Joseph were limited to some direction over his household responsibilities. Second, Joseph's language suggests that Potiphar may have specifically warned Joseph of this possibility, because Joseph said to her, "neither hath he {Potiphar} kept back any thing from me but thee, because thou art his wife" (Gen. 39:9).

Potiphar's wife was not dissuaded and continued to pursue Joseph. When he fled her grasp, he left his garment in her hand. She promptly "called unto the men of her house, and spake unto them saying, 'He came in unto me to lie with me, and I cried with a loud voice: And . . . he left his garment with me, and fled'" (Gen. 39:14-15)

Although we have no specific information about Egyptian laws regarding seduction and rape, the other codes of the ancient world are reasonably uniform about married women. Since the action took place in her house, she had to resist and provide evidence of resistance. Otherwise she would be presumed guilty of misconduct.[4] In this case Potiphar's wife had both Joseph's garment and her own rousing of the household as the necessary evidence.

To both her servants and later to Potiphar, she referred to Joseph as the "Hebrew" whom Potiphar had brought in "to mock us" (Gen. 39:14, 17), suggesting that she was playing on the natural jealousy of the other servants who had seen a newcomer rapidly assume a trusted position with Potiphar.

Confronted with the garment, witnesses who heard his wife scream, and his wife's anger, Potiphar's "wrath was kindled" (Gen. 39:19). He sent Joseph to prison.

Even with our limited understanding of Egyptian law, this seems like light punishment for attempted rape of the wife of a high-ranking official of the Egyptian government. An instructive Egyptian folk tale from the thirteenth century B.C., about two or three hundred years after Joseph's period, concerns two brothers, Anubis and Bata. Anubis was married, and Bata came to work for him on his farm. One day as they were out planting in the field, Anubis sent Bata to the house to get more seed. Not wishing to make more than one trip, Bata took a huge load. Anubis's wife admired his physical strength and suggested he spend an hour in bed with her. Appalled, Bata told her never to say such a thing again and he would not mention anything about it.

The unnamed angry wife ingested some fat and grease to make herself sick and to look as if she had been beaten. When her husband came home, she told him that Bata had propositioned her and that when she had refused he had beaten her so she would not tell. She asked him to kill Bata so that he would not try to rape her again. Anubis was enraged and waited in ambush at the shed for Bata. As Bata brought the cows into the shed, the animals warned him of Anubis's intent, and Bata was able to escape.

After a long chase Bata and Anubis talked at a distance. Bata convinced Anubis of his innocence, and Anubis after returning home slew his wife and threw her body to the dogs.[5] If this story embodies any accepted Egyptian legal principle, death may have been the penalty for attempted rape.[6] Perhaps Potiphar was less than convinced by his wife's evidence. In the biblical story, Joseph eventually rises to become chief minister of Egypt, but the wife of Potiphar is not heard from again.

Asenath

We know almost nothing about Asenath except that she was the daughter of Potipherah priest of On and that she bore Joseph at least two sons, Manasseh and Ephraim. However, her marriage to Joseph tells us something of Joseph's status at the time, and her importance to Israel cannot be underestimated.

Prior to their meeting, Joseph had been three years in prison. However, he had been elevated to a position of administrative leadership over all the prisoners (Gen. 39:22). After interpreting dreams for two prisoners, Joseph was asked to interpret the dreams of Pharaoh. Pharaoh was so impressed by Joseph and his interpretations that he made him prime minister, second only to Pharaoh himself. Did this elevation free Joseph? Not in itself. But Joseph was given an Egyptian name, Zaphnathpaaneah (41:45), which was an act of naturalization[7] and manumission,[8] since a non-debtor Egyptian could not be enslaved in Egypt.

Even more compelling evidence that Joseph was naturalized is found in the story of his encounter with his brothers when they had come seeking additional food from Egypt. Joseph invited them to eat with him at his home (Gen. 43:25) but ate at a separate table "because the Egyptians might not eat bread with the Hebrews: for that is an abomination unto the Egyptians" (v. 32).

Additional evidence of his free status is his marriage to Asenath, daughter of Potipherah. Potipherah was no relation to Potiphar but a priest of the sun god On and member of the

122

highest caste.[9] Such marriages were not consummated with slaves. Asenath's husband was free by royal decree and a ruler in Egypt under Pharaoh.

Asenath bore Joseph at least two sons.[10] Manasseh and Ephraim were adopted by Jacob on his deathbed and together given the firstborn birthright or double portion land inheritance that Jacob bestowed on their father.[11]

Of Asenath's two sons, Ephraim and Manasseh, Jacob said, addressing Joseph, "And now thy two sons, Ephraim and Manasseh, which were born unto thee in the land of Egypt before I came unto thee into Egypt, are mine; as Reuben and Simeon, they shall be mine" (Gen. 48:5). Later, during the blessing that he pronounced on them, Jacob reiterated this new relationship: "God, before whom my fathers Abraham and Isaac did walk, the God which fed me all my life long unto this day, the Angel which redeemed me from all evil, bless the lads; and let my name be named on them, and the name of my father Abraham and Isaac; and let them grow into a multitude in the midst of the earth" (vv. 15-16).

It is clear from these two passages that Jacob made an oral contract adopting Ephraim and Manasseh as his sons who would thereafter receive Joseph's land inheritance. Thus Asenath, an Egyptian, became a mother in Israel and the mother of the birthright sons.

Notes

1. G. J. Wenham, "Leviticus 27:2-8 and the Price of Slaves," *Zeitschrift fur die Alttestamentliche Wissenschaft* 90 (1978): 265; C. F. Keil and F. Delitzsch, *Commentary on the Old Testament in Ten Volumes* (Grand Rapids, MI: William B. Eerdmans Publishing Company, 1985), 1:337.

2. The Hebrew word for "officer" is *saris* meaning "eunuch." The word is of Akkadian origin from a time when most key court

officers were eunuchs, but there is no conclusive evidence that the Egyptian officers themselves were eunuchs. R. L. Harris, G. L. Archer, Jr., and B. K. Waltke, eds., *Theological Wordbook of the Old Testament* (Chicago: Moody Press, 1980), 634-35.

3. Isaac Mendelsohn, *Legal Aspects of Slavery in Babylonia, Assyria and Palestine* (Williamsport, PA: Bayard Press, 1932), 57-61.

4. "If a man seizes a woman in the mountains, it is the man's crime and he will be killed. But if he seizes her in (her) house, it is the woman's crime and the woman shall be killed. If the husband finds them, he may kill them, there shall be no punishment for him." Hittite Law 197, in E. Neufeld, *The Hittite Laws* (London: Luzac & Co. Ltd., 1951), 56; Middle Assyrian Law A 12, in G. R. Driver and J. C. Miles, *The Assyrian Laws* (Oxford: The Clarendon Press, 1935), 387; Code of Hammurabi 130, in G. R. Driver and J. C. Miles, eds., *The Babylonian Laws*, 2 vols. (Oxford: Oxford University Press, 1968), 2:53; Deut. 22:23-24.

5. James B. Pritchard, *Ancient Near Eastern Texts* (Princeton, NJ: Princeton University Press, including Supplement, 1969), 23-25.

6. In Egypt adultery was known as "the great sin"; see E. A. Speiser, *Oriental and Biblical Studies: Collected Writings of E. A. Speiser*, eds. J. J. Finkelstein and Moshe Greenburg (Philadelphia: University of Pennsylvania Press, 1967), 76. As in all ancient Near East jurisdictions, adultery was a capital crime. According to Keil and Delitzsch, Egyptian law punished attempted adultery by 1,000 blows with a rod and a severer penalty for rape of a free woman; see *Commentary on the Old Testament*, 1:345.

7. *Commentary on the Old Testament*, 1:352.

8. Mendelsohn, *Legal Aspects of Slavery*, 1932), 44.

9. Keil and Delitzsch, *Commentary on the Old Testament*, 1:352.

10. Jacob adopts only these two, and any others Joseph might have were to belong to Joseph (Gen. 48:6).

11. No one knows what vision Jacob had of his descendants' future, but giving one tribe (Joseph) a double allotment of land may have increased jealousy among the other tribes. Perhaps this diffused the issue.

124

VIII.

DAVID'S HOUSEHOLD

Michal

Michal was the younger of two daughters of Saul, the first king of Israel (1 Sam. 14:49). Michal loved David, and Saul determined to use this to his advantage to encourage David to risk his life against the Philistines. Through agents Saul urged David to "be the king's son-in-law." David demurred: "Seemeth it to you a light thing to be a king's son-in-law, seeing that I am a poor man, and lightly esteemed?" Saul responded to this polite protestation by sending word back through his servants: "The king desireth not any dowry {*mohar* or "bride-price"}, but an hundred foreskins of the Philistines, to be avenged of the king's enemies" (v. 25).

Was this a bride-price? Fathers could demand whatever bride-price they felt was reasonable in a traditional marriage, but the surviving examples of contracted marriage are all fairly ordinary transactions involving property or the groom's adoption. Nor are there any examples of royal marriage contracts where the proposed spouse was not also royal or at least noble. Hence Saul's proposal stands without recorded precedent in the ancient world. The biblical record reports the offer without comment, so it is difficult to determine the sentiment of Saul's

125

people at this unusual bride-price. Perhaps since Saul was Israel's first king, a certain amount of lattitude was expected. This arrangement seems familiar because many fairy tales and ancient myths use the similar structure of the quest, often with the goal of slaying a great enemy or bringing a desired good to the kingdom with the hand of the king's daughter being either a primary or secondary reward. David had already fulfilled such a quest in slaying Goliath. But Merab had been withheld from him and given to another man. Now Saul was requiring a second quest.

David must have realized it would be fruitless to point out the unfairness of the bargain. In fact he appeared to be delighted with this offer: "It pleased David well to be the king's son-in-law: and the days were not expired" (1 Sam. 14:26). There was a time limit set on delivery of the foreskins, and so David sprang into action, organizing a band of men to help with the scrimmage (v. 27). He seems to have had little fear of death or little worry that he could not fulfill the requirement. In fact they brought in twice the required amount—two hundred foreskins. "And Saul gave him Michal his daughter to wife" (v. 27). Even if the foreskins represented a bride-price, there was no mention of a dowry which would have been unnecessary in a metronymic marriage.[1]

For a time David was reconciled with Saul. But after he led the Israelites to another resounding victory over the Philistines, Saul's jealousy was kindled and he sought to kill David (1 Sam. 19:8). Michal helped David escape Saul's assassins by delaying them until David had left through a window (vv. 12-14). She then defended herself to her father by saying that David had threatened to kill her if she did not help him (v. 17). It is possible that by the laws of metronymic marriage, she owed a higher duty to her father than to her husband.

Further evidence that the marriage was metronymic is the mutual use of kinship terms. Several years later David found

126

Saul sleeping in a cave near the Dead Sea and cut a section from Saul's clothing. He confronted Saul with the evidence from a distance: "Moreover *my father*, see, yea, see the skirt of thy robe in my hand: for in that I cut off the skirt of thy robe, and killed thee not, know thou and see that there is neither evil nor transgression in mine hand, and I have not sinned against thee; yet thou huntest my soul to take it" (1 Sam. 24:11; italics added.) Saul called back: "Is this thy voice, *my son* David? . . . Thou art more righteous than I: for thou hast rewarded me good, whereas I have rewarded thee evil" (vv. 16-17; italics added).

During the several years of forced estrangement, Saul divorced Michal from David and married her to another man (1 Sam. 25:44). The basis for Saul's right to do this is not known. It could be that he defined David's flight as abandonment. According to Middle Assyrian Law, women abandoned for five years without support were free to remarry.[2] Perhaps Saul simply asserted his authority as king.

David did not accept the divorce, but he was powerless to prevent either it or Michal's remarriage. During the several years while he was a rebel warrior in Judah, he married two women, Abigail and Ahinoam (1 Sam. 25:42-43). As king of Judah he would add four more wives (2 Sam. 3:3-5). During negotiations with Ishbosheth, Saul's successor-son, David demanded that Michal be returned to him. Ishbosheth agreed and took her from her second husband Phalti or Phaltiel, who wept and pled fruitlessly for her return (v. 16).

The account does not record Michal's feelings at this time, but as part of David's harem her status among the wives is uncertain. Even if her separation from David and her divorce occurred against her will, her second husband evidently loved her tenderly. At best she must have had mixed feelings about being reunited to David.

Perhaps she returned to him unwillingly, or perhaps their

marital relationship deteriorated over time because of the competition with David's plural wives. Her feelings are not recorded at this point, but later, on the day of David's greatest triumph when he united Israel and brought the Ark of the Covenant to Jerusalem, Michal watched him celebrating and "despised him in her heart" (2 Sam. 6:16). When David returned to his house, Michal accused him of "shamelessly uncover[ing]" himself to dance in the streets (v. 20). He responded by banishing her from the marital chamber (vv. 22-23). Their first union, a metronymical marriage, was revoked by a despotic father/king. Their second union, a traditional marriage between a king and a daughter of a king, fared no better.

Bathsheba

Bathsheba could not resist the charms of her king and committed a capital crime by sleeping with him. It all began when David took a restless stroll on his rooftop one evening and happened to look down into his neighbor's courtyard where Bathsheba was bathing. She was "very beautiful to look upon" (2 Sam. 11:2), and the enchanted David inquired about her. She was the wife of Uriah, one of David's thirty military commanders, and the granddaughter of Ahithophel, privy counselor to David.

David knew that Uriah was away at war, laying siege in his behalf to the town of Rabbah (Amman). Apparently he did not hesitate but promptly "sent messengers, and took her; and she came in unto him, and he lay with her . . . and she returned unto her house" (2 Sam. 11:4).

Ancient legal codes are uniform in their condemnation of adultery, which they define as consensual sexual relations with a married woman by a man other than her legal husband. A married man would not be guilty of adultery if his sexual partner were unmarried. This double standard was apparently based on a woman's childbearing role. According to this rationale, ensuring that a woman had sexual access only to her husband would guarantee that a man's heir was his biological child.

Under the Code of Hammurabi, Middle Assyrian law, and Hittite law, the wronged husband was judge and executioner. Whatever punishment he determined for his wife was pronounced by the state upon her lover. If the husband killed his wife, her lover was also killed. If she was disfigured or publicly humiliated, so was he. If she was not punished, he was also set free.[3] Under the laws of Israel, adultery was considered a moral crime against the community. Therefore the legal authorities, not the husband, adjudicated such cases (Deut. 22:24; Ezek. 16:40). The only prescribed penalty for adultery in Israel was death (Deut. 22:22).

The Bible does not say whether the liaison between David and Bathsheba continued beyond this first encounter. But whether they had one or several encounters, Bathsheba became pregnant. This was a clear-cut case of adultery by both parties. It is not clear whether Bathsheba offered any resistance to David's proposal, but in any case under the terms of Deuteronomy 22:22, "they shall both of them die, both the man that lay with the woman, and the woman."

Bathsheba's story provides an example that those who have power over law refuse to be subject to it. David was the ultimate judge, the one who could condemn or reprieve from death. He brought her husband Uriah home and twice tried to send him home to have relations with Bathsheba to make him think the child was his. When these efforts failed David ordered his field commander Joab to put Uriah in the fiercest part of the battle and then to withdraw from him, leaving him to be killed. Thus Uriah, a military hero and Hittite convert to Israel, died.[4]

Some time later Nathan the prophet told David that he knew of a rich man who had great herds and flocks, while a neighbor had only one ewe lamb that he loved and had raised with his own children so that it "was unto him as a daughter." One day a traveler visited the rich man, who took the poor man's lamb and served it to the traveler for supper (2 Sam. 12:1-4).

David was livid and swore that "the man that hath done this thing shall surely die . . . because he had no pity" (2 Sam. 12:6-7). Then Nathan revealed to David, "Thou art the man," and cursed him: "Now therefore the sword shall never depart from thine house; because thou hast despised me, and hast taken the wife of Uriah the Hittite to be thy wife. Thus saith the Lord, Behold, I will raise up evil against thee out of thine own house, and I will take thy wives before thine eyes, and give them unto thy neighbour, and he shall lie with thy wives in the sight of this sun. For thou didst it secretly: but I will do this thing before all Israel, and before the sun" (vv. 10-12). As predicted, David's old age would be blighted by murder, incest, insurrection, and scandal. His ten concubines would be sexually humbled in a public tent by his son Absalom (16:22).

Bathsheba married David after her period of mourning had passed. Shortly thereafter she gave birth to their son (2 Sam. 11:27). The infant died soon thereafter in spite of a seven-day fast by David (12:14).

Bathsheba bore David four additional sons, Solomon, Shimea, Shobab, and Nathan (1 Chr. 3:5). Solomon became the most successful king in the history of Israel. Bathsheba rose to the throne of queen-mother of Israel.

Tamar: Daughter of David

One of the first events recorded after Nathan's condemnation of David is the narrative of Tamar and her brothers, Amnon and Absalom. This is a story of incestuous rape leading to fratricide.

Tamar was the daughter of David and his wife Maacah, daughter of Talmai, king of Geshur in Syria. She and her full brother Absalom were renowned for their beauty. Amnon was the oldest son of David and Ahinoam and was thus a half-brother to Tamar. He was heir-apparent to the throne of Israel, but his lust for Tamar destroyed him.

Amnon's passion for Tamar was so frenzied that he fell sick (2 Sam. 13:2). He consulted with his friend and cousin Jonadab, who schemed to trap Tamar in Amnon's bedroom. Taking advantage of Tamar's trusting nature, they asked her to come and nurse Amnon because he was sick. When she consented Amnon asked her to cook him some food.

Once Amnon and Tamar were alone, he threw her on his bed. She begged him eloquently not to rape her, pleading with him instead to ask their father for permission to marry: "My brother, do not force me; for no such thing ought to be done in Israel: do not thou this folly. And I, whither shall I cause my shame to go? and as for thee, thou shalt be as one of the fools in Israel. Now therefore, I pray thee, speak unto the king; for he will not withhold me from thee" (2 Sam. 13:12-13). But Amnon raped and brutalized her, and threw her into the street (2 Sam. 13:15).

She immediately tore her clothes and put ashes of mourning on her head. Her brother Absalom instantly deduced what had happened, "Hath Amnon thy brother been with thee?" (2 Sam. 13:20). He counseled Tamar to say nothing, took her to his own house, and spent the next two years ignoring Amnon's existence while plotting his revenge, "for Absalom hated Amnon, because he had forced his sister" (v. 22).

Under law, Amnon should have offered to marry Tamar. While marriage among brothers and sisters, including half-brothers and sisters, was prohibited in the Mosaic code (Deut. 27:22; Lev. 18:11), it was a common practice among the pharaohs of Egypt and therefore not without precedent among

131

royalty. Tamar felt that "this evil in sending me away is worse than the other" (2 Sam. 13:16).

King David, probably because of the notoriety of his own sins, took no action in this tragic affair. Amnon was not required to marry Tamar nor to pay compensation to her. We hear no more of Tamar except the poignant pronouncement that she "remained desolate in her brother Absalom's house" (2 Sam. 13:20).

Absalom took his revenge two years later. He invited Amnon to a sheep-shearing festival, and when Amnon was happily drunk, Absalom had him killed. Fearing for his life, Absalom then fled to Geshur and lived with his grandfather for three years.

David ultimately forgave Absalom. Perhaps Tamar's standing in the family and her culture was also restored by Absalom's vengeance.

David's Concubines

While king, David was married to eight named wives and ten unnamed concubines. At the time of Absalom's rebellion, when David discovered that Absalom had substantial support (2 Sam. 15:13-14), he fled Jerusalem to avoid a massacre, leaving his ten unnamed concubines in charge of the palace. Absalom recruited Ahithophel, grandfather of Bathsheba and chief counselor to David. This counselor had an impressive reputation for wisdom, and upon consolidation of his power in Jerusalem Absalom asked Ahithophel what he should do next. His advice "was as if a man had inquired at the oracle of God" (16:23). He advised Absalom to have intercourse with his father's concubines. Politically his advice had a great deal of merit. As he explained to Absalom, "And all Israel shall hear that thou art abhorred of thy father: then shall the hands of all that are with thee be strong" (v. 21). Ahithophel was

132

advising a step that would make reconciliation with David impossible.

Also, when a king died and another was crowned in his place, the former king's wives became those of the new king, if for no other reason than to continue their accustomed support. Sexual relations were permitted, except with the new king's own mother. The widows could never marry anyone else once they had been married to the king.[5] For this reason Adonijah, David's fourth son by Haggith, signed his death warrant when, after David's death, he sought to marry Abishag, David's last wife (1 Kings. 2:13-25).

Absalom accepted Ahithophel's advice and publicly asserted his kingship: "So they spread Absalom a tent upon the top of the house; and Absalom went in unto his father's concubines in the sight of all Israel" (2 Sam. 16:23).

David was ultimately victorious over Absalom, who was slain. When he returned to the palace, David placed the ten concubines in separate accommodations where they were housed, fed, and clothed. But never again was he intimate with them: "So they were shut up unto the day of their death, living in widowhood" (2 Sam. 20:3). A married woman who consented to sexual relations was guilty of adultery, a capital offense. That they survived David's return to power would suggest that they were unwilling participants (Gen. 39:14).

The Widow of Tekoah

The widow of Tekoah may not have been a widow at all. In all likelihood she was an intelligent and delightful fraud. Certainly the story she told was legally sound and touched the heartstrings of her king. She appeared before King David three years after Absalom had fled into exile for arranging the murder of his half-brother Amnon (2 Sam. 13:29). Joab, David's commander-in-chief, knew David pined for his son but was reluctant to call him home. Therefore Joab arranged for a certain woman known to us as the "Widow of Tekoah" to tell David a story that paralleled his own—of one son who killed a brother yet was loved and needed by his parent.

It is possible the widow's story was true. But I believe the story was Joab's creation, and he brought the woman from distant Tekoah (south of Bethlehem) to make her tale more difficult to verify.

The woman reported that her two sons had quarreled in a field. One killed the other. The relatives demanded that the slayer, called the "heir" (2 Sam. 14:7), be killed under the law of blood revenge (Num. 35:15-28). The widow bewailed the fact that the family would destroy her husband's name from off the earth. David accepted her story and assured her that he would issue an order protecting the son (v. 8).

The story was believable. The widow obtained her support through the inheritance that her sons had received from their father. Now one son was dead and the second was in jeopardy. The family insisted that the slayer be killed according to the law of blood revenge (Num. 35:15-28). But if the second son were killed, the name of her husband would be lost, the lineage terminated, and she would lose her position as mother or matriarch because would have no posterity.

Also, she was not an heir of the estate.[6] When the last son died, the property would go to the next heir or nearest kinsman—either a brother or nephew to her husband who was presumably among those clamoring for the death of her surviving son. Such an heir would have an obligation to support the widow, but this is a position far removed from that of matriarch with a surviving posterity.

David's assurance that he would intervene to protect the son lay fully within his powers. Cities of refuge had been established to protect killers from the law of blood revenge who were guilty of less than first-degree murder—the equivalent of manslaughter or accidental death.

If the story had been real, the widow's son would have been saved, her husband's name perpetuated, and her current standard of living secured. As it was David virtually summoned back to Jerusalem, under cloak of royal protection, the son who would eventually mount a rebellion against him and defile his concubines.

Notes

1. John Van Seters, "Jacob's Marriages," *Harvard Theological Review* 62 (1969): 386.

2. Middle Assyrian Law A 36, in G. R. Driver and J. C. Miles, eds., *The Assyrian Laws* (Oxford: The Clarendon Press, 1935), 403.

3. "If a man has taken a man with his wife (and) charge (and) proof have been brought against him, both of them shall surely be put to death; there is no liability therefor. If he has taken and brought (him) either before the king or before the judges (and) charge (and) proof have been brought against him, if the woman's husband puts his wife to death, then he shall put the man to death; (but) if he has cut off his wife's nose, he shall make the man a eunuch and the whole of his face shall be mutilated. Or, if he has allowed his wife to go free, the man shall be allowed to go free." Middle Assyrian Law A 15, in Driver and Miles, *The Assyrian Laws*, 389; see also Code of Hammurabi 129, in G. R. Driver and J. C. Miles, eds., *The Babylonian Laws*, 2 vols. (Oxford: Oxford University Press, 1968), 2:51; Hittite Law 198, in E. Neufeld, *The Hittite Laws* (London: Luzac & Co. Ltd., 1951), 57.

4. William Smith, *A Dictionary of the Bible* (Grand Rapids, MI: Zondervan Publishing House, 1972), 722.

5. C. F. Keil and F. Delitzsch, *Commentary on the Old Testament in Ten Volumes* (Grand Rapids, MI: William B. Eerdmans Publishing Company, 1985), 3:32.

6. See chap. 9.

IX.

THE INHERITANCE RIGHTS OF WIVES

United States common law does not consider wives or more correctly widows to be heirs of their husbands. However, all states have statutes providing for a widow's right to take a portion of her husband's estate (usually one-third) for her support during her lifetime.

Nor were widows considered heirs in biblical times. Some narratives describe situations in which a widow was poorly provided for and demonstrate her courage in the face of significant obstacles. What claims, if any, did a widow have on her husband's estate? What facilities of disposition were available to husbands to ensure their wives' care after their death?

The Code of Hammurabi is the only ancient legal code that clearly describes two situations in which a widow may become an heir. If a soldier had been given land and then was killed in battle, his son inherited the land, but if the son was too young to administer it, the soldier's wife became heir to one-third of the land "in order that his mother may rear him."[1]

In the second case, if a husband had not provided a marriage-gift (*nudunnum*), his wife became an heir equal with her children (sons) and received a life estate in the family house.[2] If she decided to leave the home by marrying another

137

man, she could take only her dowry. In other words she retained her heirship and life estate in the home only if she remained a widow in her husband's home. Furthermore, her only heirs were her children, and whatever she did inherit had to be kept for them. She could not dispose of it during her lifetime.

If a husband gifted property to his wife while he was alive and left a "sealed document with her,"[3] the gifted property would be hers at least for life, since her sons were her heirs. In an Old Babylonian marriage contract, a man married a widow who already had three sons, and the contract stipulated property including a house, field, and orchard which would belong to the wife. The sons were designated as the heirs with the oldest son taking a preferential share.[4]

The law so favored sons as heirs that it was common to challenge any other form of transfer, but property by gift from husband to wife could not be reclaimed by heirs after the husband's death. During a widow's lifetime, she could appoint any of her children to administer the property, but at her death they shared equally in her estate.[5] There was no firstborn double portion or special privilege in a mother's estate.

In another case described in Hammurabi's code, a free-woman married a slave and brought her dowry to their union. They then built up a joint estate through their mutual efforts. Upon the death of the husband, the wife took her dowry plus one-half of the estate, which she was required to hold in trust for her children. The owner of the slave took the other half as his ownership interest in the slave.[6]

The Middle Assyrian laws were a little less kind to wives and, except for one fairly obscure situation, only affirmed a wife's right of support. If a husband died and "assigned [a wife] nothing in writing," the wife could live in whatever house of her sons she chose.[7] All of her sons had an equal obligation of support. If she was a second wife and had no sons, she could live with one of her husband's sons by another wife, and they would all be obligated to support her. If she married one of her husband's older sons by another wife, only he had the obligation of support.

In another case, if a husband died while living with his brothers on the undivided estate of their deceased father and the husband had no son, his brothers could claim a return of any jewelry he had given his wife during their marriage. Title to all property remained in the estate. If the couple had sons, they would inherit the jewelry. If the husband had owned the jewelry outright (if it was not a part of the undivided estate) and there were no sons, then the widow would be sole heir to the jewelry.[8] In other words, under Middle Assyrian law a wife/widow had a right of support and a narrowly construed right to retain gifts received from her husband during his lifetime.

Neo-Babylonian law dating from about 600 B.C. permitted a widow to control her dowry plus any gifts her husband had given to her during her lifetime. If she did not have a dowry, the law provided one. In this sense she was not an heir but had a statutory dowry right. If she had no children, she was free to remarry. If she had children, she could remarry but would have only a usufruct in the property received from her husband, which would be distributed to her sons upon her death. If a woman had children by her second husband, they shared equally in her dowry and marital gifts with the children of her first husband.[9]

Nuzi wills were written perhaps seven hundred years before Neo-Babylonian laws. In one will, the husband Unaptae appointed his wife Sakutu guardian over his minor daughter Silwaturi by another woman. The daughter inherited all of her father's estate, and after she reached legal age, the will required her to support and care for her stepmother and give her a proper burial.

139

The husband wrote into his will a particularly harsh clause designed to prevent his wife from placing any of the estate at jeopardy: "If Sakutu, my wife, remarries, [my] brothers shall kill Sakutu."[10] We assume that this clause applied only during Sakutu's guardianship. After the daughter reached majority and took control of the estate, the wife would, one assumes, be free to take her dowry, leave, and remarry if she chose.

From Elephantine, a Jewish community on an island in the Nile River in the fifth century B.C., we find marriage documents in which the wife was sole heir of her husband's estate if he died without children.[11] Women, at least in Elephantine, generally enjoyed almost full equality with men in matters of property and obligations.[12] However, in matters of inheritance, the rights of wives in their husbands' estates were assured by legal transfer such as contract, will, or gift, not under laws of intestacy.

There is no law or statute in the Mosaic code which deals with a widow's rights or lack of rights to inherit or obtain property from her husband's estate. But two stories, those of Ruth and Naomi and of Tamar, explicitly address the problems faced by widows.

Ruth and Naomi

The narrative of Ruth and Naomi is about land. When Elimelech left Bethelem, he sold the family farm. When Naomi returned with Ruth, she apparently did not consider the possibility of recovering her husband's land. However, one evening, after Ruth had returned from gleaning in the fields of Boaz, Naomi shrewdly realized there was a complex correlation between redemption of land and levirate marriage for Ruth. They put a plan of action together that assured their own well-being as well as continued posterity for their husbands.

The story of Ruth and Naomi traces its beginnings to a

famine in Judah which forced a Hebrew couple, Elimelech and Naomi, and their two sons, Mahlon and Chilion, to leave Bethlehem for Moab east of the Jordan River and the Dead Sea. In the course of time, the father died and the brothers married Moabite women—Mahlon married Ruth, and Chilion married Orpah (Ruth 1:4). After ten years of marriage, the brothers both died, leaving their wives childless.[13]

After hearing "how that the Lord had visited his people [Israel] in giving them bread" (Ruth 1:6), Naomi decided to return to Bethlehem where presumably her kinfolk lived. Furthermore Israel practiced the law of gleaning—a unique cultural practice designed to provide for widows and orphans without other means of support:

> And when ye reap the harvest of your land, thou shalt not wholly reap the corners of thy field, neither shalt thou gather the gleanings of thy harvest.
> And thou shalt not glean thy vineyard, neither shalt thou gather every grape of thy vineyard; thou shalt leave
> them for the poor and stranger: I am the Lord your God
> (Lev. 19:9-10; see also 23:22).
> When thou cuttest down thine harvest in thy field, and hast forgot a sheaf in the field, thou shalt not go again to fetch it: it shall be for the stranger, for the fatherless, and for the widow: that the Lord thy God may bless thee in all the work of thine hands.
> When thou beatest thine olive tree, thou shalt not go over the boughs again: it shall be for the stranger, for the fatherless, and for the widow.
> When thou gatherest the grapes of thy vineyard, thou shalt not glean it afterward: it shall be for the stranger, for the fatherless, and for the widow (Deut. 24:19-21).

As Naomi set out "on the way to return unto the land of

Judah" (Ruth 1:7), she urged her daughters-in-law to return to their parents' houses. Their fathers would have been responsible for their support, and we know specifically that Ruth's father was still alive (2:8, 11).[14] Naomi invoked a blessing upon them "that ye may find rest, each of you in the house of her [second] husband," but they refused to leave her, desiring to return with her "unto thy people" (1:10).

Orpah and Ruth had probably accepted the God of Israel and the Hebrew way of life. Naomi reminded them, however, that she could not promise them family position or security, for she had no more sons to perform the levirate duty. All they could do was to share her lot: "Why will ye go with me? are there yet any more sons in my womb, that they may be your husbands? Turn again, my daughters, go your way; for I am too old to have an husband. If I should say, I have hope, if I should have an husband also to night, and should also bear sons; Would ye tarry for them till they were grown? would ye stay for them from having husbands? nay, my daughters; for it grieveth me much for your sakes that the hand of the Lord is gone out against me" (Ruth 1:11-13).

Orpah was persuaded, kissed Naomi good-by, and returned "unto her people, and unto her gods" (Ruth 1:15). But in a strong, stirring statement, Ruth affirmed her love for Naomi and the God of Israel: "Intreat me not to leave thee, or to return from following after thee: for whither thou goest, I will go; and where thou lodgest, I will lodge: thy people shall be my people, and thy God my God" (v. 16). Ruth had faith enough in Naomi and the God of Israel to forsake the security of her home and travel to Bethlehem.

Shortly after their arrival, Ruth decided to glean for food. She happened upon the field of Boaz, a kinsman of Elimelech. As she worked, he watched her and learned who she was from his foreman. Boaz already knew of Naomi's return to Bethlehem and of the convert who had followed her (Ruth

142

2:11). He praised Ruth: "The Lord recompense thy work, and a full reward be given thee of the Lord God of Israel, under whose wings thou art come to trust" (v. 12). He then helped make his blessing a reality by inviting her to dinner and instructing his servants to leave a little extra in the fields for her. Ruth managed to glean an ephah (twenty-two liters) of barley for herself and Naomi.

As Ruth returned home she met Naomi and told her of her success. As Ruth recounted the day's activities, Naomi realized that she and Ruth had an opportunity available through a combination of the customs of land redemption and levirate marriage. Pleased and excited by Ruth's report, Naomi thanked God for this kindness to them, for Boaz was "one of our next kinsmen" (Ruth 2:20). In fact, the Hebrew *goel* (next kinsman) means "he who has the right to redeem." Naomi understood that Boaz had the right to redeem their ancestral lands. And if they could prevail upon him to perform the levirate duty and provide an heir for Mahlon, such an heir would provide them security.

A redeemer or next kinsman could redeem ancestral land lost to a family through foreclosure or other circumstance. The land of Israel belonged to Jehovah (Lev. 25:23) and was given to the Israelites to be used by them in perpetuity or until they ceased to serve God. Each tribe had its own land, and within its tribal inheritance, families were assigned their legacies by lot (Jos. 13-19). Through Moses God commanded that lands never be permanently alienated from the family. Thus land had religious significance to Israelites.

If a landholder were forced to sell his or her land, he or she would first approach the next of kin, who had the right of first refusal to buy the land.[15] If the land was foreclosed upon to satisfy an unpaid debt, the family still retained a right of redemption, and if that did not suffice, a jubilee right of return (Lev. 25:13).

Under the rule of redemption, a landowner could at any time repay the balance of his debt to the creditor and regain his land. The balance owed was calculated according to the number of crops the land would produce before the year of jubilee (Lev. 25:15-16). If the landowner was unable to redeem his land, he could prevail upon a relative (next of kin) to purchase it for him and return him to his estate. Beyond the desire to preserve family honor and avoid public shame, there would appear to be little incentive for a next of kin to redeem the land of his relative unless that relative had no heirs, in which event the land would revert to the next of kin upon the relative's death.

The redemption right was inheritable and remained with the family as long as an heir survived. Such a surviving heir reacquired family lands in the jubilee year, a "sabbath of sabbaths" that occurred every fifty years (seven times seven years plus one year). On a given day in that year, all land was to revert to its original family owner. Thus in theory each dispossessed family could repossess its ancestral home at least once every fifty years. No wonder genealogies were important: "If thy brother be waxen poor, and hath sold away some of his possession, and if any of his kin come to redeem it, then shall he redeem that which his brother sold. And if the man have none to redeem it, and himself be able to redeem it; Then let him count the years of the sale thereof, and restore the overplus unto the man to whom he sold it; that he may return unto his possession. But if he be not able to restore it to him, then that which is sold shall remain in the hand of him that hath bought it until the year of jubilee: and in the jubilee it shall go out, and he shall return unto his possession" (Lev. 25:25-28).

Since both Ruth's husband and her father-in-law were deceased, she was legally a widow, free to marry whomever she pleased. With Naomi's guidance, Ruth chose a path that would raise up seed to her deceased husband and redeem the family

144

lot. In the evening, she went to the threshing floor, keeping out of sight. "When Boaz had eaten and drunk, and his heart was merry, he went to lie down at the end of the heap of corn: and she came softly, and uncovered his feet, and laid her down" (Ruth 3:7). Awakened and startled to find someone sharing his bed on the corn, Boaz asked who she was. Ruth answered, "I am Ruth thine handmaid: spread therefore thy skirt over thine handmaid; for thou art a near kinsman" (v. 9).

The language is clearly sexual.[16] The invitation to "spread therefore thy skirt over thine handmaid" is a direct reference to marital intercourse.[17] The phrase "for thou art a near kinsman" in effect informed Boaz of his levirate duty and asked him to consummate it. Ruth could not compel Boaz to marry her, but she had the legal right to ask him. Therefore while his "heart was merry" from a harvest celebration, Ruth asked him to complete the duty.

However, neither she nor Naomi appear to have realized that Boaz was not the nearest next of kin. Boaz, who was better informed, told Ruth he would be willing to be her husband if it were not for the one nearer kinsman (Ruth 3:12). Boaz apparently refrained from being intimate with Ruth until he had a chance to confront the nearest next of kin.[18]

Boaz told Ruth that he would meet with the unnamed relative in the morning. And if he proved unwilling to become Ruth's husband, Boaz would then be free to marry her and be the redeemer (goel) of Elimelech's and Mahlon's family lands. He then suggested she stay the night and sent her home with six measures of barley early the next morning "before one could know another" (Ruth 3:14). Obviously he did not want it known that she had spent the night near him ("Let it not be known that a woman came into the floor"), but J. M. Sasson suggests that it may not have been any more discreet for a young woman to walk home in the early morning, heavily laden with grain, a common form of currency.[19] Was Boaz concerned

145

about her safety if she went home alone late at night? Was he concerned about his reputation if he accompanied her home?

As the day's activity began, Boaz went to the gate where contracts were made and witnesses from the town elders were easily found. Here he expected the kinsman to pass on his regular morning exit of the walled city to his fields. When the kinsman came Boaz asked him to sit down. Boaz arranged for ten witnesses. Because two or four would have been sufficient, the large number indicates that Boaz considered this transaction important. He then explained, "Naomi, that is come again out of the country of Moab, selleth a parcel of land, which was our brother Elimelech's" (Ruth 4:3). "Brother" here is probably a generic term of kinship.

This statement establishes that it was possible for women to inherit land or at least inherit the right to deal with family lands but probably not in their own interest. Where widows were left land by contract or gift, it was always with the condition that the children would receive the land at the mother's (or widow's) death.[20] But in Naomi's case the land was presumably first left to her sons Mahlon and Chilion. But then they died childless. Did they gift or bequeath the land to Naomi? Or did she automatically inherit the land because her sons died childless?[21]

There are many theories about how Naomi came to own the land.[22] But in the absence of an heir, the law would probably allow for the birth of a potential heir before final disposition of the land.[23]

Boaz informed his relative of his preferential right of redemption, assuring him that if he would not redeem it, then Boaz would. This would include responsibility for supporting Naomi, but the land would produce considerably more than Naomi's support and the land title would vest in him after her death. The kinsman, perhaps predictably, agreed. Then Boaz played his trump card. He told him about "Ruth the

Moabitess," who would also require support, with the additional responsibility of performing the levirate duty and raising an heir who would of course inherit the land instead of the kinsman (Ruth 4:5).[24]

The kinsman refused, "lest [he] mar [his] own inheritance" (Ruth 4:6). Depleting his estate to buy land and then raising up an heir to take possession was more than the kinsman was prepared to do.

Deuteronomic law established a specific procedure in such cases. If the kinsman did not accept the widow's invitation to perform the levirate duty, then before she was free to seek remarriage with a partner of her choice, the widow had to arraign the reluctant brother-in-law before the elders in the city gate and there accuse him of refusing to raise up an heir. The elders would interview the recalcitrant one. If he continued to refuse, the widow was to remove his shoe and spit in his face, saying, "So shall it be done unto that man that will not build up his brother's house" (Deut. 25:7-9). Thus the brother-in-law was publicly shamed.[25]

What is the significance of the shoe? Some suggest that because the shoe was sometimes used in transferring property titles, the brother-in-law gave up any rights that he might have had to his brother's property.[26] Whatever the legal significance, by "loosing the shoe" the kinsman relinquished his responsibility as a kinsman to produce an heir for his brother. Boaz had been careful to send Ruth home so that she would not be present at the gate and also to let the kinsman know that he himself was willing to be a redeemer and husband. Thus the kinsman would be spared a scene of public shaming.

As Boaz had hoped, the kinsman responded by giving his shoe to Boaz and with it his rights to the land redemption and also to the levirate duty. For this reason he gave the shoe to Boaz and not to Ruth. Boaz then made a formal declaration before the witnessing elders: "Ye are witnesses this day, that I have bought all that was Elimelech's, and all that was Chilion's and Mahlon's of the hand of Naomi. Moreover, Ruth the Moabitess, the wife of Mahlon, have I purchased to be my wife, to raise up the name of the dead upon his inheritance, that the name of the dead be not cut off from among his brethren" (Ruth 4:10).

As a result of their union, Ruth conceived and bore a son who was given the name of Obed, "and Naomi took the child and laid it in her bosom, and became nurse unto it" (Ruth 4:16). Was Obed their only child? The record is silent. There is no dictum in the law against additional offspring in the levirate union. If Ruth were Boaz's sole wife, then it seems reasonable to suppose that the marriage would have been a normal connubial relationship, except that the firstborn Obed would have had special inheritance rights to Elimelech's property and Boaz would have had guardianship rights in that estate during Obed's minority. In the event of more than one child of the levirate marriage, only the firstborn belonged to the deceased husband. All others including daughters belonged to the levirate husband.

The primary purpose of levirate marriage was to produce a male heir. In the case of Ruth, it is clear that this son became heir to the estate of Mahlon, his legal father, even though the final verses of the book of Ruth pronounce the genealogy of generations between Pharez, the levirate child of Judah and Tamar, and David—through Boaz not through Mahlon. Obed was grandfather of king David and a forebear in the royal lineage of Jesus.

Tamar: Mother of the Jews

This story begins with Judah, a leader among Jacob's sons and the initiator of Joseph's betrayal (Gen. 37:26). Knowing that his father never believed the fabricated story of Joseph's demise[27] and unable to bear his shame and remorse, Judah left Hebron and traveled west down the Shephelah to Adullam. Here he married an unnamed Canaanite woman, a daughter of Shua, and adopted Canaanite customs and laws. Judah and the daughter of Shua had three sons: Er, Onan, and Shelah.

Following his patriarchal prerogative, Judah selected a Canaanite wife named Tamar for Er, his firstborn. We know only that Er fathered no children with Tamar and that God took him for his wickedness (Gen. 38:7-8). Er's death shattered Tamar's marital expectations and eliminated the status, support, and protection for which she had married. In early biblical times, a woman who married a firstborn son expected to bear a son who would take his father's place in the family hierarchy as the chief heir of his father's estate. Being the wife of a firstborn son or leader in a patriarchal community meant that she would be mother of a future community leader. Such position was both socially and economically prestigious. The wife of a patriarch or leader became a matriarch or chief wife and was leader in the extended family: as her husband was chief man, she was chief woman. Her husband inherited at least a double portion of his father's estate, twice as much as any other heir. This inheritance assured him of added respect and family and community leadership and would have been appealing to some women.

Tamar had recourse to the law of levirate marriage. In Canaanite practice a son born to the levirate union bore the deceased husband's name, for such a son inherited all the deceased husband's property and continued as a link in an unbroken genealogical chain as though he were the biological son of the deceased husband.

It was also in Judah's best interest to retain Tamar in the family. If Tamar entered into a levirate marriage and bore children, she would help maintain the numerical strength and economic integrity of the family, despite Er's untimely death.

Tamar's marital obligation continued as long as the father-in-law was alive. She was not declared a widow, able to "go whither she pleases," until both her husband and father-in-law were dead. None of the laws mentions a preference in the order of kin, nor did it matter whether the brother or father was already married. However, if the story of Tamar is typical, we may assume that older brothers were preferred over younger brothers, who were in turn preferred over the father.[28] In order then, Onan was preferred over Shelah, who was preferred over Judah.

The initiative in arranging a levirate marriage for Tamar belonged to Judah. If he did not provide a son or himself as a husband, then Tamar had the right to demand that one of them perform his duty. This prerogative was based on custom, not civil or criminal statutes enforceable in a court of law. Therefore a brother-in-law could accept or reject the request of his sister-in-law without fear of legal retribution, although he probably had less choice about his father's request.[29] If he refused the sister-in-law, his only punishment was being held up to public shame through a legal shoe-removing ritual known in Jewish law as *halitzah*.

Judah arranged for Onan, his second son, to marry Tamar. Though it was considered honorable for the brother to impregnate his brother's widow and thereby preserve his brother's name, the death of Er had naturally increased Onan's share of the family inheritance. Furthermore, Onan would now inherit the firstborn's share, which was double that of the other sons. If Tamar bore a legal son for Er, then Onan, the biological though not the legal father (for purposes of the inheritance), would lose this doubled estate. Perhaps for this reason, Assyrian law cited above left the choice of levirate marriage to the father-in-law rather than to the brother.

When Judah, Tamar, and Onan reached an agreement, the levirate marriage became effective upon consummation.

150

There was no need for a new dowry or a new marriage contract: all the arrangements of the first marriage between Er and Tamar remained in effect. Since she was Er's chief wife, she retained chief wife status with Onan. If Onan was already married—his marital status is not clear—Tamar's chief wife status would pertain only to Er's estate.

Knowing that he was next in line for the blessings of the firstborn, Onan did not openly defy his father, an act for which he could have been disinherited. Instead, he conspired to deceive Judah and defraud Tamar. During the connubial act, through *coitus interruptus,* he "spilled {his semen} on the ground, lest that he should give seed to his brother. And the thing . . . displeased the Lord: wherefore he slew him also" (Gen. 38:9-10).

Judah's only remaining son, Shelah, was not "grown" (Gen. 38:11), indicating that he had not reached puberty. The minimum marriageable age under Middle Assyrian law was ten.[30] Judah asked Tamar to live in her father's house as a widow. Tamar's father had the legal obligation of support "till Shelah my son be grown" (v. 11). This condition constituted an oral contract that Judah would have Shelah perform the levirate duty when he was of age. Tamar kept her part of the agreement by returning to her father's house.[31]

An unspecified amount of time passed, but it must have exceeded puberty for Shelah, for Tamar became aware that Judah was keeping Shelah from her. She devised a stratagem, and on a day when Judah was going to shear his sheep at a certain location, she disguised herself as a lay sacral prostitute.

Cultic prostitutes were women who offered their services to the public and donated the proceeds to the temple. In early times, according to Herodotus, sacral prostitution was expected of all Babylonian women at least once in their lifetime.[32] The practice came from the myth of a male deity such as the Canaanite god Baal, the god of rain, fertilizing his lover or wife/sister Anat, the earth goddess, which brought forth food. A scholar notes: "It is known that feasts of the preexilic period were accompanied by ritual fornication with the magic intention of securing rich crops and increase of herds. Judah's visit to a hierodule at that time of year was a predictable ritually pre-scribed act."[33] Judah had apparently adopted this custom at some point during his stay in Adullam.[34] He was, moreover, recently widowed (Gen. 38:12).

Judah saw her "covered with a vail," which evidently was a part of her costume that signalled her status as a cult prostitute, and asked permission to visit her. They agreed upon a kid as the fee. Since Judah had no animals with him, Tamar required as a pledge or guarantee his signet ring, bracelets, and staff. Judah willingly entrusted these valuable objects to her, an indication of the esteem given these prostitutes. Later Judah sent his friend Hiram to deliver the kid, another indication that he was not ashamed of his activity. But the "prostitute" had disappeared.

Three months later Tamar's pregnancy became publicly known. Recall that she was the childless widow of Er. She and her father-in-law Judah had agreed that Shelah would perform the levirate duty when he became of age. So Tamar was under the levirate obligation to Shelah, a legal status similar to a betrothal. Her pregnancy was prima facie evidence of adultery since Shelah had had no relations with her.

Even though Judah had asked Tamar to return to her father's house while she waited for Shelah, Tamar still came under Judah's patriarchal authority. Legal systems of the time left capital punishment for certain crimes against the family in the hands of the patriarch.[35] Hearing of the pregnancy and even before confronting Tamar, Judah ordered, "Let her be burnt" (Gen. 38:24). It is not known what the Abrahamic/patriarchal traditional punishments for adultery were. Reuben lost his birthright (49:4), and Bilhah's punishment if any is not recorded. However, burning is a penalty found in Babylonian law though not for adultery.[36] The usual Babylonian penalty for adultery was death by drowning. Burning may have been a Canaanite penalty for adultery of which we have no record.

Tamar appeared at a "judicial hearing" and presented Judah's signet, bracelets, and staff, all personal items conspicuously known to be Judah's, and identified their owner as the father of her child. Judah understood the legal ramifications of Tamar's evidence and dropped the charge and punishment of death, admitting, "She hath been more righteous than I; because that I gave her not to Shelah my son" (Gen. 38:26).

Judah was not guilty of adultery because he was a legal consort. Thus even if Tamar had acted improperly, the child would have been legitimate. Judah "knew her again no more" (Gen. 38:26) indicating that although she had acted correctly, he had no intention of pursuing a relationship beyond the levirate duty.

During the births of Tamar's twin sons, whose conception was linked to the rights of the firstborn, another interesting question about firstborn sons emerges. When the hand of one infant came out first, the midwife tied a scarlet thread on it. But the other child, Pharez, was actually the first to draw breath. Zarah was born second, with the scarlet thread on his wrist. Which was the firstborn? Ancient legal codes are silent on this issue, but Jewish law dating from about A.D. 200 held that the one whose head emerged first was the firstborn, even though it might then withdraw—a physiologically unlikely event—and be preceded by the other twin.[37] Under most modern legal systems, an infant does not become a "person" until he or she takes a breath. Whatever the law, Pharez, the first to emerge or draw breath, was the firstborn, surpassing even Shelah since Pharez was heir to Er under the law of levirate marriage.

We do not know why Tamar was so thoroughly resolved to

bear a son for her husband Er. Perhaps she wished to solidify her position as matriarch in the house of Judah. As mother of Pharez, firstborn of Judah, she was the tribal matriarch. When the chronicler lists those who accompanied Jacob to Egypt at the behest of Joseph, her sons Pharez and Zarah are included. Tamar is not mentioned, but neither are other women. If she were still alive, we can assume that she would have been there.

Tamar's twins became heirs of their grandfather's estate at birth. We do not know when Judah died. But if Pharez and Zarah were still minors, Tamar would have become administrator of their inheritance in Judah's estate until the boys attained majority. From that point on they would have been responsible for her support.

Notes

1. Code of Hammurabi 29, in James B. Pritchard, *Ancient Near Eastern Texts* (Princeton, NJ: Princeton University Press, including Supplement, 1969), 167.

2. "If her [deceased] husband did not give her a marriage-gift, they shall make good her dowry to her and she shall obtain from the gods of her husband's estate a portion corresponding to (that of) an individual heir; if her children keep plaguing her in order to make her leave the house, the judges shall investigate her record and place the blame on the children, so that woman need never leave her husband's house; if that woman has made up her mind to leave, she shall leave to her children the marriage-gift which her husband gave her (but) take the dowry from her father's house in order that the man of her choice may marry her." Code of Hammurabi 172, in ibid., 173; see also Code of Hammurabi 171, in ibid.

3. "If a seignior, upon presenting a field, orchard, house, or goods to his wife, left a sealed document with her, her children may not enter a claim against her after (the death of) her husband, since the mother may give her inheritance to that son of hers whom she likes, (but) she may not give (it) to an outsider." Code of Hammurabi

150, in ibid., 172.

4. Raymond Westbrook, "Old Babylonian Marriage Law," Vol. 1, Ph.D. diss., University of Michigan, Ann Arbor, 1982, 218.

5. G. R. Driver and J. C. Miles, *The Babylonian Laws*, 2 vols. (Oxford: Oxford University Press, 1968), 1:269.

6. Code of Hammurabi 176, in Pritchard, *Ancient Near Eastern Texts*, 174.

7. Middle Assyrian Law A 46, in ibid., 184.

8. Middle Assyrian Law A 25-26, in G. R. Driver and J. C. Miles, *The Assyrian Laws* (Oxford: Clarendon Press, 1935), 397, also 195.

9. Neo-Babylonian Laws 12-13, in Pritchard, *Ancient Near Eastern Texts*, 197.

10. J. Paradise, "A Daughter and Her Father's Property at Nuzi," *Journal of Cuneiform Studies* 32 (Oct. 1980): 196.

11. Reuven Yaron, *Introduction to the Law of the Aramaic Papyri* (Oxford: Clarendon Press, 1961), 69.

12. Ibid., 43.

13. The names of the story's main characters are so parallel that coupled with the deaths of the sons at exactly ten years, one suspects scribal intervention in the interests of symmetry:

Elimelech: God is king	Naomi: the pleasant one
Mahlon: sickly	Chilion: weakly
Ruth: the friend	Orpah: turned back
Boaz: the pillar	Obed: serving

14. The KJV has Naomi recommending that her daughters-in-law return "each to her mother's house," but Septuagint manuscripts say "father's house," and the Syriac manuscript has "your parents." Edward F. Campbell, Jr., *Anchor Bible, Ruth* (Garden City, NY: Doubleday, 1975), 60nf.

15. H. H. Rowley, "The Marriage of Ruth," *Harvard Theological Review* 40 (1947): 89.

16. William Gesenius, *A Hebrew and English Lexicon of the Old Testament*, eds. F. Brown, S. R. Driver, and C. A. Briggs (Oxford: Clarendon Press, 1976), 163. Anthony Phillips, "The Book of Ruth—Deception and Shame," *Journal of Jewish Studies* 37 (Spring

1986): 14. See also Edward F. Campbell, "The Hebrew Short Story: A Study of Ruth," in *A Light unto My Path; Old Testament Studies in Honor of Jacob M. Myers*, eds. Howard N. Bream, Ralph D. Heim, and Carey A. Moore (Philadelphia: Temple University Press, 1974), 96.

17. C. F. Keil and F. Delitzsch, *Commentary on the Old Testament in Ten Volumes* (Grand Rapids, MI: William B. Eerdmans Publishing Company, 1985), 2:484. See also Ezek. 16:8.

18. Beyond the husband's brothers, the nearest of kin in order would be the father, father's brothers, father's brother's sons, then the father's father and on down his line. We do not know how far in the order of succession a widow could go to find the next of kin. We know that Ruth's husband's brother and his father were deceased. We also know that Boaz was one step removed from being the next of kin. If Boaz and the nearest kinsman had been brothers, it would have been simpler to explain their relationship thus. Consequently it is more likely that they were paternal cousins or sons of paternal granduncles with the nearest kinsman in some position of seniority.

19. J. M. Sasson, *Ruth* (Baltimore, MD: Johns Hopkins University Press, 1979), 95.

20. J. Paradise, "A Daughter and Her Father's Property at Nuzi," *Journal of Cuneiform Studies* 32 (Oct. 1980): 195.

21. D. R. G. Beattie, "The Book of Ruth as Evidence for Israelite Legal Practice," *Vetus Testamentum* 24 (July 1974): 254.

22. "If a woman whose husband is dead does not go forth from her house on her husband's death, (and) if her husband has assigned her nothing in writing, she shall dwell in a house belonging to her sons where she chooses; her husband's sons shall provide her with food; they shall enter into a covenant for her for (the provision of) her food and her drink as (for) a bride whom they love. If she is a second (wife and) she has no sons, she shall dwell with one (of her husband's sons and) they shall provide her with food in common; if she has sons (and) the sons of the former (wife) do not agree to provide her with food, she shall dwell in a house belonging to her own sons where she chooses, (and) her own sons too shall provide

her with food and she shall do their work. But if indeed among her sons (there is one) who has taken her (as his spouse), he [who takes] her (as his spouse) [shall] surely [provide her with food and her (own) sons] shall [not] provide her with food." Middle Assyrian Law A 46, in Driver and Miles, *The Assyrian Laws,* 415; see also Code of Hammurabi 29, 39, 172, in Pritchard, *Ancient Near Eastern Texts,* 167, 168, 173; see also Neo-Babylonian 12, in ibid., 197.

23. Keil and Delitzsch, *Commentary on the Old Testament,* 2:489.

24. Dale Manor phrased this situation using an interesting parallelism, "Although it may be an oversimplification, a summary of the Ruth narrative and the go'el/yabham [redeemer/brother of deceased childless husband] relationship is that in a levirate marriage, the land goes with the woman; in a go'el situation, the woman goes with the land"; see Manor, "A Brief History of Levirate Marriage As It Relates to the Bible," *Restoration Quarterly* 27 (1984): 138). In other words, if the nearer kinsman acted as a redeemer over the land, he also had to act as a redeemer of the name of the dead and raise up an heir to his deceased kinsman or vice versa.

25. According to David Daube, we should not underrate the seriousness of such public shame: "No doubt a man branded as 'he that hath his shoe loosed' was avoided by the better citizens, excluded from higher offices and not trusted in any business transactions." See Daube, "Consortium in Roman and Hebrew Law," *Juridical Review* 62 (1950): 78. Thereafter the widow had no further responsibility to her first husband's family.

26. T. Thompson and D. Thompson, "Some Legal Problems in the Book of Ruth," *Vetus Testamentum* 18 (1968): 93. A friend, John Tvedtness, adds that the Hebrew for sandal (na'al) is probably a wordplay with (nahal) meaning "inheritance." The medial consonants are both pharyngeal fricatives, one voiced and the other unvoiced.

27. According to one very convincing treatise, Jacob never believed Reuben's evidence but was constrained to accept it by the rules of prima facie evidence. See especially Genesis 44:28 where Judah quotes Jacob as saying, "Surely he [Joseph] is torn in pieces; and I saw him not since." See David Daube, *Studies in Biblical Law*

(New York: KTAV Publishing House, 1969), 9.

28. "[If], while a woman is still living in her father's house, her husband died and . . . she has no [son, her father-in-law shall marry her to the son] of his choice . . . or if he wishes, he may give her in marriage to her father-in-law. If her husband and her father-in-law are both dead and she has no son, she becomes a widow; she may go where she wishes." See Middle Assyrian Law A 33, in Pritchard, *Ancient Near Eastern Texts*, 182. While there is no Canaanite code as such, this section parallels the fact situation of the Tamar narrative. Cf. Deut. 25:5.

29. Anthony Phillips, "The Book of Ruth—Deception and Shame," *Journal of Jewish Studies* 37 (Spring 1986): 3-4.

30. Middle Assyrian Law 43, in Pritchard, *Ancient Near Eastern Texts*, 184.

31. It is clear that Judah did not release Tamar from her levirate duty at this time. He had already lost two sons and made no secret of his fear that he would also lose Shelah (Gen. 38:11). Now he stood to lose a daughter-in-law and her dowry as well. Clearly Judah needed time to assess his predicament.

32. Edwin M. Yamauchi, *Cultic Prostitution in Orient and Occident* (Verlag Butzon & Bercker Kevelaer, 1973), 216.

33. Michael C. Astour, "Tamar the Hierodule," *Journal of Biblical Literature* 85 (1966): 193.

34. About six hundred years later, the sons of the prophet Eli would introduce this practice at the Lord's tabernacle at Shilo (1 Sam. 2:22). Certainly they knew of the Deuteronomic prohibition against sacral prostitution: "Thou shalt not bring the hire of a whore, or the price of a dog {male sacral prostitute}, into the house of the Lord thy God for any vow: for even both these are abomination unto the Lord thy God" (Deut. 23:18). Judah, embracing the Canaanite culture several generations before Moses, had no such proscription.

35. See Middle Assyrian Law A 15, in Driver and Miles, *The Assyrian Laws*, 389. See also Hittite Law 198, in E. Neufeld, *The Hittite Laws* (London: Luzac & Co. Ltd., 1951), 57. See also Code of Hammurabi 129, in Driver and Miles, *The Babylonian Laws*, 2:51.

36. See Code of Hammurabi 110, in ibid., 2:45.

37. Bekoroth 46b, in I. Epstein, ed. and trans., *The Babylonian Talmud* (London: Soncino Press, 1948), 318.

X.

THE DAUGHTERS OF ZELOPHEHAD

The story of the daughters of Zelophehad raises interesting questions about the rights of women. What expectations did they have regarding inheritance? Why would they want to be heirs? Could they be heirs in the absence of sons? Historically males were obligated to support women and children and therefore became primary heirs of the land and property of their parents. Women had the responsibility to create families by bearing and nurturing children. This could be best accomplished in a stable and secure environment to be provided by the father and husband. Both roles were recognized and regulated by law.

In some ways women were better off than heirs. They could use their interest in their father's estate (usually one-tenth of its value) when they needed it most—at the beginning of their married life. A present receipt of a future interest such as a dowry could be much more valuable than an heir's uncertainty of waiting for the death of a benefactor. A wife was supported by her husband in the stable environment of his parental home and could thus turn her full attention to her children.

Ideal expectations, however, were not always reality. How did the ancients deal with family inheritance when there were no sons? The story of Zelophehad and his daughters provides some interesting insights.

Zelophehad was not the first father to sire only daughters, but he was one of the most famous. He was the second great-grandson (fifth generation) of Manasseh, son of Joseph (Jos. 17:1-3). He followed Moses out of Egypt and died in the wilderness before reaching the promised land. He had five daughters: Mahlah, Noah, Hoglah, Milcah, and Tirzah (Num. 27:1).

Apparently they did not expect an inheritance from their father. But one day after their father's death, according to Jewish tradition, Moses was discussing levirate marriage within the daughters' hearing.[1] It occurred to them that if a childless widow could preserve her husband's name through an heir provided by levirate marriage, an heir who would inherit the deceased husband's lands, justice demanded that a way be found to preserve the name of an honorable man who had only daughters. If daughters could inherit those lands, they could thus perpetuate his name and thereby honor him. They faced an additional incentive, for as a firstborn son, Zelophehad would have himself received a double portion from his father.[2]

The daughters brought their petition before Moses, Eleazer (son of Aaron) the priest, and the whole congregation of Israel and their leaders (Num. 27:2). They described their father to Moses as faithful to the God of Israel. He had not participated in the rebellion of Korah, and his only "sin" was that he died without having a son (v. 3). "Why should the name of our father be done away from among his family, because he hath no son?" they asked. "Give unto us therefore a possession among the brethren of our father" (v. 4). Concerned with the perpetuation of their father's name, they insisted that they be allowed to inherit the land and by a new legal fiction to preserve the name of their father—the land would be known as the land of a *daughter* of Zelophehad

None of the tribes of Israel had yet received a land inheritance. Perhaps despite the Jewish tradition in Baba Bathra to the contrary, all Israel was gathered together to plan the distribution of the land and not to discuss levirate marriage. According to the narrative, this would be a more logical setting for the daughters' petition. However, Moses was said to be present in the court (Num. 27:2), and inheritances were not thought to have been distributed until after Moses' death, when Joshua and the tribes of Israel had subdued the land (Jos. 13-19). At that time the land was assigned by lot to individuals among the tribes. Each of Zelophehad's daughters received two lots because their father was a firstborn son (17:5). Therefore, a plausible explanation is that the daughters had actually sought to participate in the original division of land inheritances after they arrived in Canaan and to have the land chosen by lot under their father's name.

Could this legal problem have been avoided if Zelophehad had thought through more carefully how to dispose of his property and to provide for his daughters? Or was it impossible at that point under the laws of Israel for a daughter to inherit from her father?

In all probability, the daughters appeared before the court of Israel sometime in the late thirteenth or early twelfth century B.C. What laws in the ancient Near East at or before these times related to the inheritance rights of daughters, even though the new Mosaic code was generally more liberal and enlightened than the codes of neighboring societies?

The Code of Lipit-Ishtar permitted daughters who became priestesses to be full heirs with their brothers.[3] A priestess served in the temple and did not receive a marital dowry. Such women thus could inherit land. Since such daughters/priestesses would never have children, their brothers became their heirs.

The Code of Hammurabi permitted a soldier to deed any

property he owned that he had not received as a gift from the king for military service to his wife or daughter.[4] The Code of Hammurabi also contained a provision permitting inheritance rights for a priestess[5] and added that a father could give his priestess daughter full power to bequeath her inheritance to whomever she wished. If the father did not provide for his priestess daughter by gift or will, the law did. Her estate automatically went to her brothers upon her death, unless she was a priestess of Marduk (the highest rank). Then she was free to do as she wished.[6] According to the Code of Hammurabi, if a father provided his daughter with a dowry at her marriage, she was no longer considered his heir.[7]

Statutes regarding inheritance rights of daughters are missing or are simply not addressed in other codes. Therefore, we can identify two principles from the two aforementioned codes: (1) If a daughter decided to forego marriage and dedicated herself to the service of the gods, she became an heir of her father; (2) if a daughter married and received her dowry from her father or her brothers, she lost heirship rights.

If we assume that similar codes applied in Israel—an assumption that can neither be proven nor disproven—we have an interesting situation presented in the parable of Job. He made his three daughters equal heirs with his seven sons (Job 42:15). Why did the author of this story think he would have been able to do this?

It was not unheard of in ancient law for daughters to become heirs. When Gudea, ruler of Lagash (a city in Sumer, part of the future empire of Babylon but before the rule of Hammurabi), published his edict to establish justice in his domain, he announced, "In the house in which there is no son, the daughter enters into the position of heiress."[8] Another Old Babylonian legal text from Nippur records, "If a man dies and he has no sons, his unmarried daughters shall become his heirs."[9]

However, another document from roughly the same period and location (the ancient Babylonian city of Sippar) notes, "There is no right of inheritance for daughters in Sippar, be they the eldest or not."[10] Although this last statement does not say whether such daughters had brothers and the text is incomplete, it appears that the inheritance rights of daughters were not uniform throughout the Near East. Even in the absence of sons, the inheritance rights of daughters appear to have been more of a benevolent aberration than a generally accepted practice.

Legal documents from Nuzi about 1300 B.C. provide additional insight. The Nuzis practiced adoption on an unprecedented scale for their time. In one Nuzi contract, a father adopted his daughter as a son for inheritance purposes: "Thus (declared) Unaptae, 'My daughter Silwaturi I have given the rank of son. . . . The entire inheritance share, in the city and in the various cities, I have given to my daughter Silwaturi, whom I had given the status of son.'"[11] We do not know whether she had any brothers. In another contract a father adopted a son and married his daughter to him, making them joint heirs—with the provision that if the son/son-in-law ever married another wife or divorced the daughter, all the inherited property would pass to the daughter.[12]

Other documents indicate that daughters were made equal heirs with their brothers.[13] In some contracts sole daughters were heirs subject to the birth of a son/brother, who then became sole heir.[14] Apparently a father could also give his daughter any gift that he wished during his lifetime or in his will, including both real and personal property.[15] Documents from other ancient communities such as Ugarit, Alalah, and Elam reveal instances where daughters inherited even when they had brothers.[16]

It is clear that fathers were generally not prohibited from making their daughters heirs. Even among adherents of the

Mosaic code, if a father wanted a daughter to inherit from his estate, he could find a way by will or gift (Jos. 15:19; Job 42:15). If he did not create a legal transfer during his lifetime, however, in most jurisdictions his daughter would not receive an inheritance, although she would have rights of dowry or maintenance.

Zelophehad's daughters argued before Moses and the other members of the court that it was unfair that they could not use their father's right to cast lots and that some provision should be made so they could inherit and preserve their father's name upon his inheritance. Moses took their petition before the Lord and received the following answer:

> The daughters of Zelophehad speak right: thou shalt surely give them a possession of an inheritance among their father's brethren: and thou shalt cause the inheritance of their father to pass unto them.
> And thou shalt speak unto the children of Israel, saying, If a man die, and have no son, then ye shall cause his inheritance to pass unto his daughter.
> And if he have no daughter, then ye shall give his inheritance unto his brethren.
> And if he have no brethren, then ye shall give his inheritance unto his father's brethren.
> And if his father have no brethren, then ye shall give his inheritance unto his kinsman that is next to him of his family, and he shall possess it: and it shall be unto the children of Israel a statute of judgment, as the Lord commanded Moses (Num. 27:7-11).

Thus, Israel's law of intestacy was changed, and daughters were added to the chain of succession, becoming second only to their brothers. If a father died with only daughters and had not provided for those daughters by will, they became his legal heirs.

Some time later other members of the tribe of Manasseh

complained to Moses that if the daughters of Zelophehad married outside the tribe, their inheritance would go with them and thus diminish the tribe of Manasseh. Clearly this ran contrary to the original purpose in giving them an inheritance (Num. 36:3). Moses agreed and amended the law so that daughters had to marry within their father's tribe to retain the land inherited (v. 8). All the daughters of Zelophehad married cousins (v. 11).

The Daughters of Lot

The daughters of Lot engaged in unusual sexual relations for which they have been both maligned and blessed. The sons they bore became the founders of nations protected by God.

God determined to destroy the city of Sodom where Lot and his family lived but sent angels who gave Lot and his family an opportunity to flee before the destruction came. Lot could not convince the husbands of his married daughters to come. But he, his wife, and his two unnamed daughters fled from Sodom shortly before "brimstone and fire" rained upon it and upon its sister city, Gomorrah (Gen. 19:24).

As they fled, Lot's wife looked back, disobeying the instructions of the warning angels, and was turned into a "pillar of salt" (Gen. 19:26). Lot and his daughters fled to a cave in the mountains where they stayed, afraid to go out because of the great destruction.

It is not clear how long they were there, but apparently they had a clear view of the desolation. They apparently concluded that the entire earth had been devastated and depopulated. Lot's eldest daughter proposed to the younger: "Our father is old, and there is not a man in the earth to come in unto us after the manner of all the earth: Come, let us make our father drink wine, and we will lie with him, that we may preserve seed of our father" (Gen. 19:31-32).

167

These women appear to have understood the principle of levirate marriage. If a man died childless, a brother or other near relative would become the widow's husband for the purpose of fathering a child to preserve the name of the deceased husband and to provide security for the wife in her old age.

The daughters of Lot apparently contemplated such a union. It would not have been a conventional levirate marriage. But they believed there were no more available worthy men of their lineage—and they justified their act by the same principles justifying levirate marriage. On consecutive nights the daughters made Lot drunk and then had sexual relations with him, the elder on the first night and the younger on the second. This did not constitute rape since a woman could not by legal definition rape a man.

Ancient legal codes prohibited fathers from committing incest with their daughters. The Old Babylonians of Hammurabi's time banished from the city fathers who committed incest with their daughters from the city.[17] The Hittites, several centuries later, would make father-daughter incest a capital crime for the father.[18]

Lot's daughters were aware that Lot could not, ethically or legally, consent to their plan to provide him with offspring, but he could not be faulted if there was no intent on his part, and no law specifically prohibited daughters from initiating sexual relations with their father.

Each of Lot's daughters bore a son. The oldest daughter called her son Moab ("from the father") and the second daughter called her son Ben Ammi ("son of my people"). These sons became the forefathers of the Moabites and the Ammonites, who were protected by God until they fell into idolatry. Moab was an ancestor of Ruth and therefore of David, Solomon, and Jesus.

Notes

1. Baba Bathra 119b, in I. Epstein, ed. and trans., *The Babylonian Talmud* (London: Soncino Press, 1948), 490.

2. Jos. 17:5; Baba Bathra 8.3, in Herbert Danby, trans. *The Mishnah* (Oxford: Oxford University Press, 1985), 376.

3. "If the father (is) living, his daughter whether she be a high priestess. a priestess, or a hierodule shall dwell in his house like an heir." Code of Lipit-Ishtar 22, in Francis Rue Steele, "The Code of Lipit-Ishtar," *American Journal of Archaeology* 52 (1948): 439.

4. "He [a soldier] may deed to his wife or daughter any of the field, orchard, or house which he purchases and accordingly owns, and he may assign (them) for an obligation of his." Code of Hammurabi 39 (see also Sec. 38), in James B. Pritchard, *Ancient Near Eastern Texts* (Princeton, NJ: Princeton University Press, including Supplement, 1969), 168.

5. "If (there is) a high-priestess a priestess or an epicene whose father has bestowed a dowry on her and has written a tablet for her (but) has not granted her written authority in the tablet which he has written for her to give (the charge of) her estate to whom she pleases and has not conceded her full discretion, (then,) after the father goes to his fate, her brothers shall take her field and her plantation (into their charge) and give her food oil and clothing according to the capacity of her share and satisfy her. If her brothers do not give her food oil and clothing according to the capacity of her share and do not satisfy her, she may give her field and plantation (in)to (the charge of) any cultivator who pleases her and her cultivator shall maintain her; she shall enjoy the field (and) the plantation (and) anything which her father gave her so long as she lives. She shall not sell (them and) she shall not use them to settle the claims of any other (person). Her inheritance belongs to her brothers." Code of Hammurabi 178, in G. R. Driver and J. C. Miles, eds., *The Babylonian Laws*, 2 vols. (1952; rprt. Oxford: Oxford University Press, 1968), 2:71.

6. Code of Hammurabi 180, 182, in ibid., 2:73.

7. "If a father has bestowed a dowry on his daughter (who is) a lay-sister, has given her to an husband (and) has written a sealed tablet for her, after the father goes to (his) fate, she shall at the division

169

not take (anything) out of the property of the paternal estate." Code of Hammurabi 183, in ibid.

8. Z. Ben-Barak, "Inheritance by Daughters in the Ancient Near East," *Journal of Semitic Studies* 25 (1980): 23.

9. Ibid.

10. Ibid.

11. J. Paradise, "A Daughter and Her Father's Property at Nuzi," *Journal of Cuneiform Studies* 32 (Oct. 1980): 189.

12. Ibid., 191.

13. Ibid., 192.

14. Ibid., 194.

15. Katarzyna Groesz, "Dowry and Brideprice in Nuzi," in *Studies on the Civilization and Culture of Nuzi and the Hurrians in Honor of Ernest R. Lacheman,* eds. M. A. Morrison and D. I. Owen (Winona Lake, IN: Wisenbrauns, 1981), 168.

16. Ben-Barak, "Inheritance by Daughters," 24-32.

17. "If a man (carnally) knows his daughter, they shall banish that man from the city." Code of Hammurabi 154, in Driver and Miles, *The Babylonian Laws,* 2:61.

18. "[If a man] sins with his mother, (it is) an abomination {capital crime}. If a [man] sins with a daughter, (it is) an abomination. If a man sins with a son, (it is) an abomination." Hittite Law 189, in E. Neufeld, ed., *The Hittite Laws* (London: Luzac & Co. Ltd., 1951), 54.

XI.

MISCELLANEOUS CASES

The Rape of Dinah

Dinah, Jacob's daughter by Leah, was naive about the customs in Shechem, where Jacob settled after escaping from Laban. Driven by curiosity, she left the security of her father's tents and went out to "see the daughters of the land." Instead she was noticed by Shechem, son of Hamor, the ruler of Shechem. Shechem took Dinah "and lay with her," but instead of considering her a one-time conquest, "his soul clave unto Dinah the daughter of Jacob, and he loved the damsel, and spake kindly unto the damsel. And Shechem spake unto his father Hamor, saying, Get me this damsel to wife" (Gen. 34:1-4).

Was this a rape or a seduction? Scholars disagree. Verse 2 reads: "Shechem. . . saw her, he took her, and lay with her, and defiled her." Josephus uses the words "defiled her by violence."[1] Louis Epstein describes her ordeal as "rape."[2] William Smith in his Bible dictionary says she was "violated by Shechem."[3] Keil and Delitzsch in their commentary say she was seduced,[4] and Alfred Edersheim calls Dinah "blameworthy."[5] However, defiled in Hebrew is "ana" meaning to "be bowed down," "afflicted," and, in the sense in which it is used

171

regarding Dinah, "humbled,"[6] which sounds more like rape than seduction.

According to Middle Assyrian laws codified a little later than this account, if a man raped an unbetrothed maiden, he could be forced to marry her and to pay a bride-price to her father. If the father did not wish to give his daughter to the rapist, he could take the bride-price and penalty and marry her to anyone he wished.[7] Such laws suggest the possibility of marriage by rape. Community pressure would be on the father to accept a nobly born son such as Shechem as a son-in-law. In the eyes of the community, Dinah would be "damaged goods" to any other other suitor.

Hamor, Shechem's father, arranged a meeting with Jacob attended by all of Dinah's brothers. Hamor asked not only for Dinah's hand in marriage for his son but also for other marriages between the families. Shechem, rather than being an unwilling bridegroom, offered to pay "what[ever] ye shall say" (Gen. 34:8-12).

At this point Jacob's sons took over the negotiations and "deceitfully" agreed to the marriage on the condition that all the men of Shechem would submit to circumcision. They all consented, believing that Jacob's prosperity would bring wealth to them and to their town (Gen. 34:23). Jacob, unaware of his sons' intentions, consented by his silence.

On the third day after the circumcisions when all the men of Shechem were too sore to defend themselves, Simeon and Levi swooped down on the town and killed them all. Dinah was already in Shechem's house, for the two brothers "took Dinah out of Shechem's house" after they had slain Hamor and Shechem. This can only mean that payment of the bride-price, which included the circumcision of Shechem, concluded a formal marriage, and Dinah had accompanied Shechem home as his bride. However, Shechem's pain would not have permitted him to consummate the marriage, and

Simeon and Levi annulled it when they killed the young groom. After Levi and Simeon had killed the males of the city, the other sons of Jacob sacked the town and took all women and children captive (Gen. 34:25, 27-29).

Jacob was angry at his sons and told them: "Ye have troubled me to make me to stink among the inhabitants of the land" (Gen. 34:30). No law prescribed death for rape of an unbetrothed maiden, not to mention destruction of a whole town—even though communal responsibility was an accepted legal principle of the times.

In anger and fear (Gen. 35:1), Jacob moved his family to Bethel and then to Bethlehem, where Rachel died (v. 19). Finally he settled in Hebron but nothing more is mentioned of Dinah in the sacred text.

Pharaoh's Daughter

Little is known about the daughter of Pharaoh—not even her name. But few people are unaware of the roll she is said to have played in adopting[8] the baby that was to become known as the preeminent Hebrew lawgiver, Moses.

Before we meet Pharoah's daughter, we are introduced to the circumstances of Moses' birth. He is said to have been born in Egypt at a time when Pharaoh had ordered the extermination of male Hebrew babies (Ex. 1:16, 19, 22). In this environment Moses was born to Amram and Jochebed, both of the tribe of Levi. Jochebed nursed Moses for three months, as long as she dared. Knowing the habits of the daughter of Pharaoh, she then put Moses into a little waterproof basket and floated him down the Nile when she knew the princess would be bathing. She left little to chance and sent Miriam, Moses' sister, to watch him from the bullrushes along the shore.

Pharaoh's daughter discovered the infant and, disobeying her father's edict, saved him. Miriam made herself known at this time and volunteered to find a wet nurse for the child (Ex. 2:7). Contract wet nursing was a common practice, especially with adopted infants.[9] The princess thus accepted the services of the Moses' biological mother. This Hebrew baby must have been quite a palace secret.

Therefore, through fortuitous circumstances, Jochebed was engaged to raise her son in his infancy and was paid wages to do so. At the end of her contract, which may have been anywhere from two to five years,[10] Jochebed returned Moses to Pharoah's daughter and "he became her son. And she called his name Moses" (Ex. 2:10). By naming him, and publicly announcing him as "her son," she would have been unmistakably adopting the child, bestowing on him all the rights and duties of a son of the daughter of Pharoah.

Zipporah

When God threatened to kill Zipporah's firstborn son because her husband Moses had failed to circumcise him, Zipporah instantly performed the rite herself with a sharp stone (Ex. 4:25). Zipporah's boldness was perhaps due in part to the fact that her marriage with Moses was a metronymic one.

One late afternoon in the desert of Midian, seven sisters, tending their flocks, were driven from the community well by other shepherds (Ex. 2:16). A stranger, an Egyptian by dress and apparently well trained in martial arts, intervened on behalf of the women and watered their flocks. When they reported this incident to their father, Jethro, he rebuked his daughters for their lack of hospitality and sent them back to invite the stranger to his tent.

Moses accepted their invitation and stayed forty years, marrying Zipporah, one of Jethro's daughters. The scriptures do not mention a bride-price or dowry, the absence of which is one evidence of metronymic marriage. Second, "Moses kept

174

the flock of Jethro his father in law, the priest of Midian" (Ex. 3:1), not under contract like Jacob, for it is never raised as an issue. Moses became a member of Jethro's household. A third indication that this was a metronymic marriage is that when God commanded Moses to go to Egypt and free Israel from bondage, Moses asked Jethro's permission: "Let me go, I pray thee, and return unto my brethren which are in Egypt, and see whether they be yet alive. And Jethro said unto Moses, Go in peace" (4:18).

After Moses had delivered Israel from bondage, Jethro brought Zipporah and their sons to Moses in the desert (Ex. 18:1-5). It appears that Jethro then terminated Moses' obligation to him as his metronymic father-in-law. Jethro returned to Midian (v. 27), and there is no record that they ever saw each other again. By relinquishing whatever rights he had, Jethro was released from the responsibility for supporting Zipporah and her two children in the harsh desert of Midian.

The Unnamed Concubine

And if a man sell his daughter to be a maidservant,
she shall not go out as the menservants do.
If she please not her master, who hath betrothed her
to himself, then shall he let her be redeemed: to sell
her unto a strange nation he shall have no power,
seeing he hath dealt deceitfully with her.
And if he have betrothed her unto his son, he shall
deal with her after the manner of daughters.
If he take him another wife; her food, her raiment,
and her duty of marriage, shall he not diminish.
And if he do not these three unto her, then shall she
go out free without money (Ex. 21:7-11).

The book of Exodus records the case of a Hebrew daughter sold by her father to another Hebrew. In this case the sale appears to have been a form of marriage arrangement. It was not uncommon for a father to arrange for a daughter under the age of puberty to join the family of another as a servant, expecting that when she reached puberty she would marry the master. The sale price then included payment for her services as a servant and a bride-price, and it may have been paid as cash or as relief for a debt owed by the father to the master.

This contract differed from a normal marriage contract because the master had options: If he decided he did not want to marry the girl, he could marry her to his son. If his son did not want to marry her, they had to set her free. Consideration was paid for the contract, but the arrangement lacked some of the requirements of a chief-wife marriage, because the daughter in those circumstances would come to the betrothal without a dowry. Therefore, she would be a concubine or secondary wife.

The daughter was not treated like a son sold into servitude. Such a son was usually sold for a specified time and then freed to pursue his life. If no agreement established a certain time for service, male slaves for debt were freed at the end of six years or at the Jubilee, whichever came first.[11] A female Hebrew slave could "not go out [free] as the menservants do" at the end of six years but after six years became betrothed to the master (Ex. 21:7).[12] If the daughter was not betrothed to the master at puberty as expected, she was to be made available for redemption, for "he hath dealt deceitfully with her" (v. 8). She could not be resold even to another Hebrew.[13] Her redeemers included her father, near kinsmen, or any suitor. They needed only to repay the master the money he had paid less the value of her service.[14]

Since the daughter had been sold into servitude, the master could betroth her to any of his sons and was then required to "deal with her after the manner of daughters" (Ex. 21:9). This appears to mean that the master would have to provide her with a dowry. Having a dowry, however, suggests that she

176

would probably have been a chief wife of the son.

The biblical statute describes a situation in which the master marries the daughter and then later marries a second wife. Because the daughter's marriage benefits were threatened, we can presume that the new wife had a higher status and was probably a chief wife. A wife's marital expectation of support included food, clothing, and an opportunity to bear children. Once a standard was set in a marriage, nothing was to be diminished. If a daughter was deprived of her marriage expectations, she could dissolve the marriage by divorcing her husband. If she did divorce him, she was not obligated to repay the bride-price or in this case the purchase-price paid her father. She was then free to remarry as she wished.

Interestingly, this concubine had a right of divorce for cause—if her support or her marital rights were diminished. It is unlikely that a chief wife had fewer rights in this regard.

Although treatment of women in the Old Testament seems harsh—to say the least—compared to modern standards, it is clear that women were protected in unsuspected ways. If a woman insisted—often through intrigue—on her rights and privileges, she could sometimes fare as well as a man. In some ways women were granted more authority, respect, and independence than today. Considering the fact that male scribes were generally responsible for transmitting these texts, it is surprising that so much remains about women outwitting and dominating men. In fact, the importance of women asserting themselves in the face of opposition may be the most instructive moral of these stories. In this sense, they are essential to preserve and understand.

Notes

1. Josephus, "Antiquities of the Jews," in *Josephus: Complete Works*, trans. William Whiston (1960; rprt. Grand Rapids, MI:

Kregel Publications, 1972), 43.

2. Louis M. Epstein, *Sex Laws and Customs in Judaism* (New York: KTAV Publishing House, Inc. 1967), 179.

3. William Smith, *A Dictionary of the Bible* (Grand Rapids, MI: Zondervan Publishing House, 1972), 146.

4. C. F. Keil and F. Delitzsch, *Commentary on the Old Testament in Ten Volumes* (Grand Rapids, MI: William B. Eerdmans Publishing Company, 1985), 1:311.

5. Alfred Edersheim, *Old Testament Bible History* (Grand Rapids, MI: William B. Eerdmans Publishing Co., 1984), 139.

6. William Gesenius, *A Hebrew and English Lexicon of the Old Testament*, eds. F. Brown, S. R. Driver, and C. A. Briggs (Oxford: Clarendon Press, 1976), 776.

7. "In the case of a seignior's daughter, a virgin who was living in her father's house, whose [father] had not been asked (for her in marriage), whose hymen had not been opened since she was not married, and no one had a claim against her father's house, if a seignior took the virgin by force and ravished her, either in the midst of the city or in the open country or at night in the street or in a granary or at a city festival, the father of the virgin shall take the wife of the virgin's ravisher and give her to be ravished; he shall not return her to her husband (but) take her; the father may give his daughter who was ravished to her ravisher in marriage. If he has no wife, the ravisher shall give the (extra) third in silver to her father as the value of a virgin (and) her ravisher shall marry her (and) not cast her off. If the father does not (so) wish, he shall receive the (extra) third for the virgin in silver (and) give his daughter to whom he wishes." Middle Assyrian Law A 55, in James B. Pritchard, ed., *Ancient Near Eastern Texts* (Princeton, NJ: Princeton University Press, including Supplement, 1969), 185.

8. Moses was an adopted son, yet the law code he developed has no provision for adoption. Following this lead modern common law has no provision for adoption. It is covered only in statutory law.

Black's Law Dictionary defines "adopt" as "to take into one's family the child of another and give him or her the rights, privileges, and duties of a child and heir" (Henry C. Black, *Black's Law Dictionary* [St. Paul, MN: West Publishing, 1968], 70). This definition fits the adoption of Moses.

9. The laws of Eshnunna dating from about 1900 B.C. contain interesting provisions concerning wet nursing. A father was required to pay a wet nurse three years' worth of barley, oil, and wool. If he did not pay the goods, he was required to pay a huge penalty of ten minas of silver for her services (Laws of Eshnunna 32, in Pritchard, 162; Laws of Eshnunna 32, in Reuven Yaron, *The Laws of Eshnunna* [Jerusalem: Magnes Press, 1969], 37, 169). Unpaid wet nurses could sell the nursling into slavery to recover their wages.

The Code of Hammurabi exposed a different problem when it imposed a penalty on the nurse who had a child die in her care. She was required by the statute to inform any new client that a child had died in her care. If she failed to do so, her breast would be amputated to prevent her from causing the death of another child; Code of Hammurabi 194, in G. R. Driver and J. C. Miles, *The Babylonian Laws*, 2 vols. (Oxford: Oxford University Press, 1968), 2:77; see also 1:406.

10. Ibid.; see also Keil and Delitzsch, *Commentary on the Old Testament*, 2B:26; they say the Israelite custom was to nurse three years.

11. M. Mielziner, *The Institution of Slavery Among the Ancient Hebrews* (Cincinnati: Bloch Printing Co., 1894), sec. 5.

12. Ibid., sec. 12.

13. Ibid., sec. 8.

14. Ibid., sec. 11.

INDEX

181